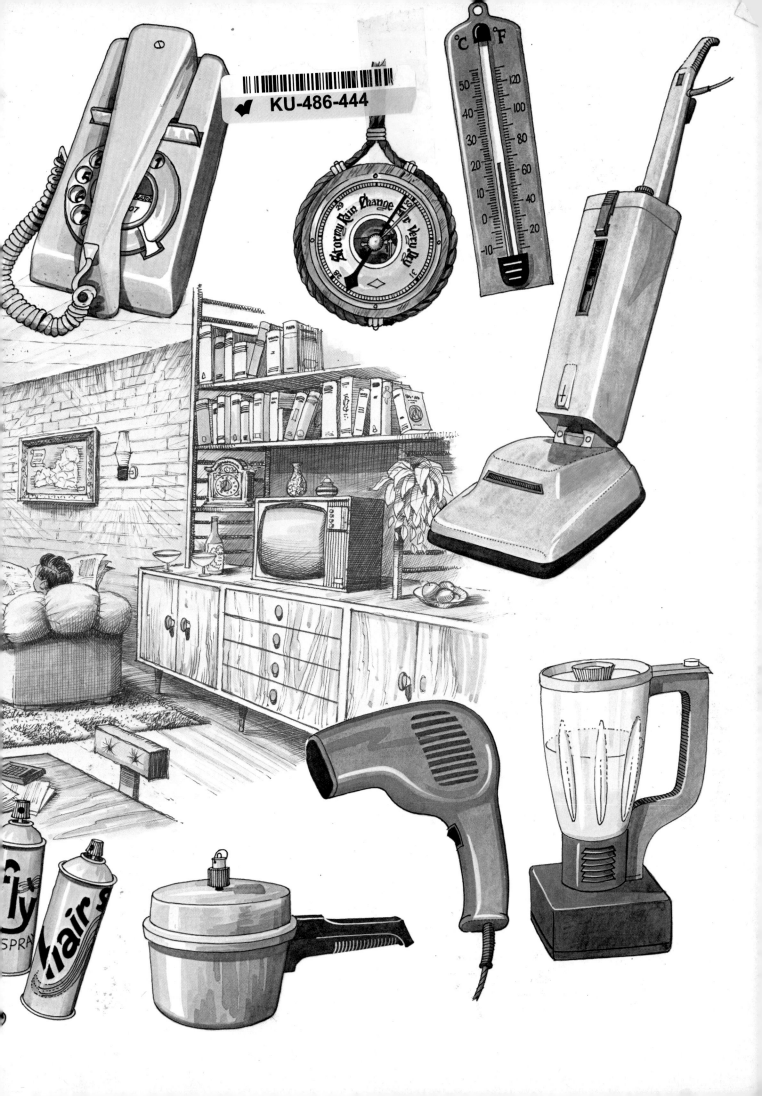

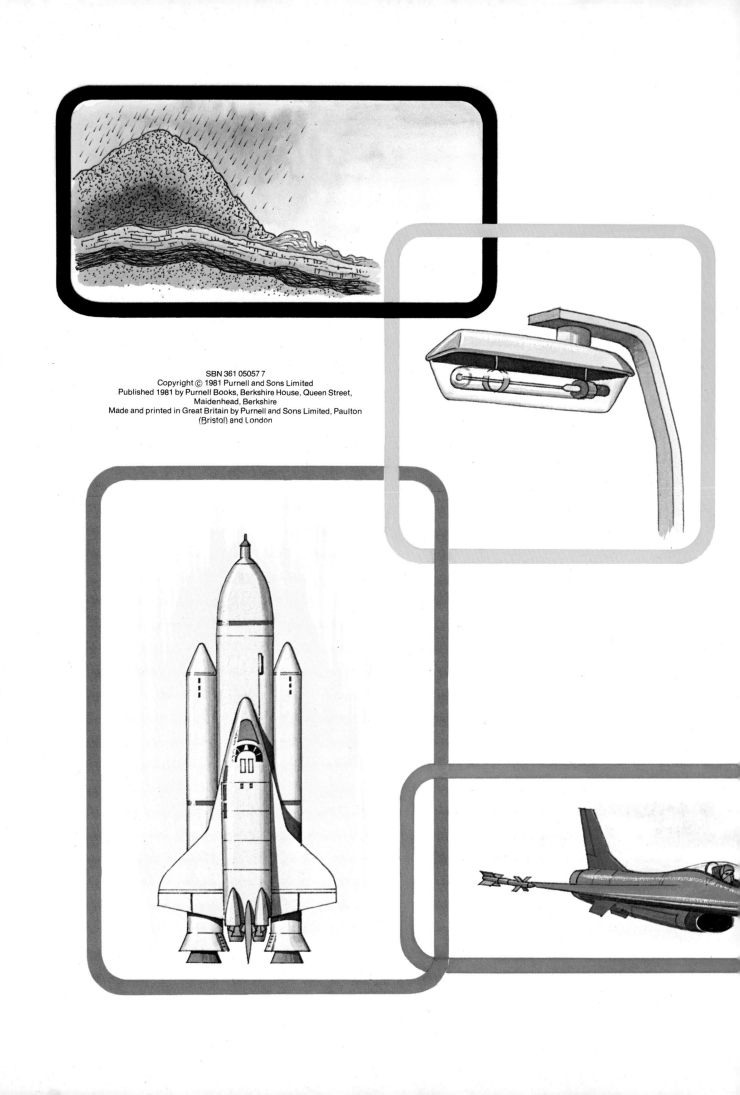

SBN 361 05057 7
Copyright © 1981 Purnell and Sons Limited
Published 1981 by Purnell Books, Berkshire House, Queen Street,
Maidenhead, Berkshire
Made and printed in Great Britain by Purnell and Sons Limited, Paulton
(Bristol) and London

# Purnell's
# FIRST
# DICTIONARY
## OF
# SCIENCE

Written by Robin Kerrod

Illustrated by Bryan Foster

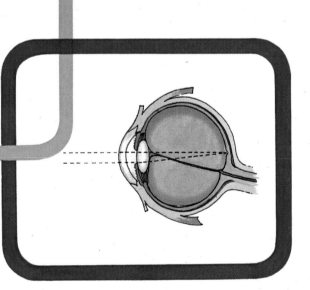

# Aa

### absolute zero
The lowest temperature that can be reached. It is about −273° C.

### acid
A chemical with a sour taste. Weak acids such as lemon juice are often harmless. Strong acids such as sulphuric acid can eat away metals and they are also deadly poisons.

### aerial
A metal rod or dish that sends out or collects radio waves. Also called antenna.

### aerosol
A cloud of fine particles.

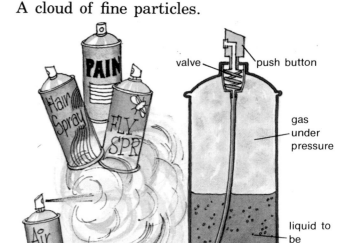

valve
push button
gas under pressure
liquid to be sprayed
aerosol can

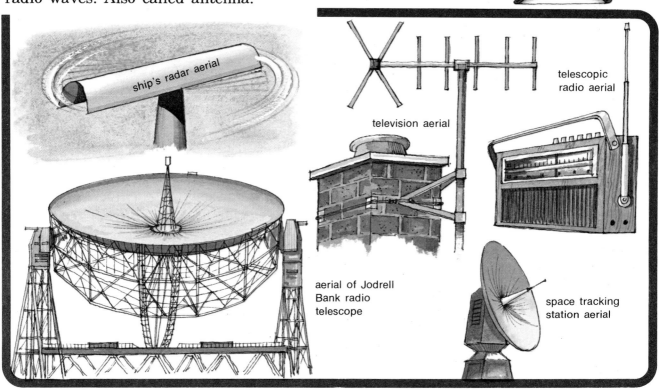

ship's radar aerial

television aerial

telescopic radio aerial

aerial of Jodrell Bank radio telescope

space tracking station aerial

### aerofoil
The shape of an aeroplane's wing, thick at the front and thin at the rear.

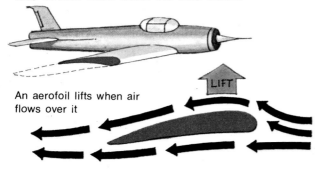

An aerofoil lifts when air flows over it

LIFT

### air
The mixture of gases in the Earth's atmosphere. It is made up mainly of nitrogen (78 per cent), oxygen (21 per cent) and argon (nearly 1 per cent). It has no colour, taste or smell. We feel it as the wind.

### air pressure
The air presses down on every square centimetre of the Earth with a weight of more than 1 kilogram. The air pressure becomes less the higher you go.

## alchemy

An early form of chemistry in which people tried to turn cheap metals into gold.

## alcohol

The substance in beers, wines and spirits that makes people merry. It is produced by the fermentation of sugars.

## alkali

A substance that is the chemical opposite of an acid. Solutions of alkalis in water often feel soapy and are good cleaning agents.

## alloy

A mixture of one metal with another or with a non-metal, such as carbon. Alloys are generally stronger than pure metals.

## aluminium

The cheapest lightweight metal. It conducts heat and electricity well.

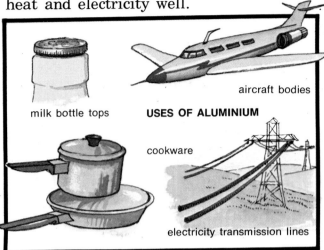

milk bottle tops

aircraft bodies

**USES OF ALUMINIUM**

cookware

electricity transmission lines

## amalgam

An alloy of a metal with mercury. Dentists use amalgams to fill teeth.

## ammeter

An instrument that measures electric current.

## anaesthetic

A substance given to a patient to prevent him feeling pain. In hospitals a *general* anaesthetic is given before and during a surgical operation. A dentist uses a *local* anaesthetic to deaden just the gums when he drills teeth.

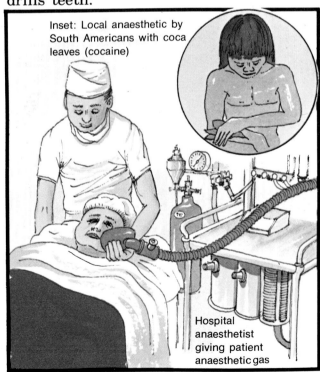

Inset: Local anaesthetic by South Americans with coca leaves (cocaine)

Hospital anaesthetist giving patient anaesthetic gas

## Andromeda nebula

One of the nearest galaxies to our own, which we can see with the naked eye. Its light takes two million years to reach us.

## antibiotic

A powerful drug that fights disease germs. It is produced from certain moulds.

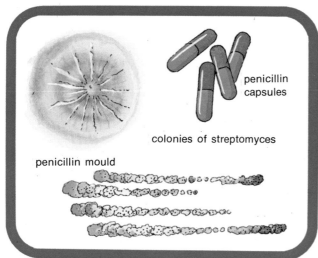

penicillin capsules

colonies of streptomyces

penicillin mould

## antifreeze

A substance added to water to prevent it freezing at the normal freezing point (0°C). Ethylene glycol is the commonest antifreeze, used in car radiators.

## antimatter

Matter whose atomic particles have opposite electric charges from normal. Anti-protons, for example, have a negative charge.

## Apollo

The spacecraft used by American astronauts to travel to and land on the Moon between July 1969 and December 1972. It was made up of three parts (modules)—one for the crew (command), one for the main equipment (service) and one for the Moon landing (lunar).

## aqua regia

'Noble water'. A mixture of hydrochloric and nitric acids which can dissolve gold.

multi-arch bridge

arch dam

## arch

A curved structure built to support a load. It is widely used above or across a gap in engineering, in building bridges and dams.

## arsenic

A chemical element whose compounds are very poisonous.

## asbestos

Rock that is found in the form of fibres which can be made into fireproof materials. These materials can then be made into such things as protective clothing for firemen and theatre safety curtains. Asbestos is also used to make roofing tiles and to insulate boilers.

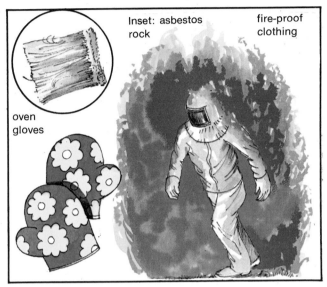

Inset: asbestos rock

fire-proof clothing

oven gloves

## aspirin

The best-known pain-killing drug, first made from coal. Its proper name is acetyl salicylic acid.

Below: the three parts of Apollo linked together

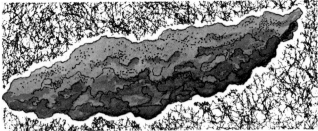

## asteroid

A tiny planet. Thousands of asteroids circle around the Sun between the orbits of Mars and Jupiter.

## astigmatism

A defect of the eye which causes blurred vision. The eye lens cannot bring all the light rays from an object to a proper focus.

## astrology

Trying to foretell the future by studying the heavenly bodies. Astrologers believe that events and people's lives are affected by the positions of the Sun, Moon and planets.

## astronaut

A traveller in space. The Russians call their space travellers cosmonauts. Yuri Gagarin (Russia) was the first man in orbit (12 April 1961).

American astronaut Edward White space walking in 1965

## astronomy

The scientific study of the heavens. Astronomers work in observatories, where they observe and photograph the heavenly bodies through telescopes. They study starlight in instruments and can tell from it how big, how hot and how far away the stars are. Astronomers now also use space satellites and probes to investigate the heavenly bodies.

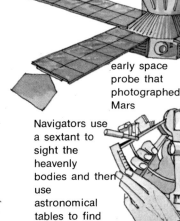

the planet Saturn as viewed through a telescope

an orrery, which shows how the planets move through the heavens

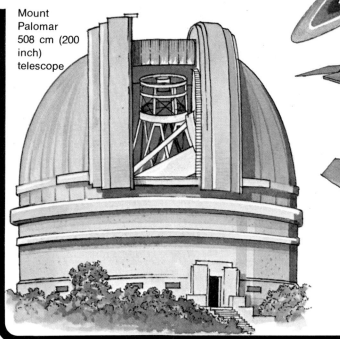

Mount Palomar 508 cm (200 inch) telescope

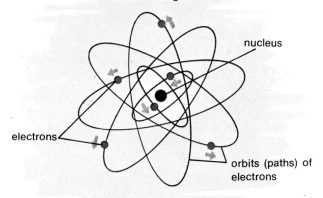

early space probe that photographed Mars

Navigators use a sextant to sight the heavenly bodies and then use astronomical tables to find their position

## atmosphere

The layer of gases around a planet. The Earth's atmosphere consists of the gas we call air. The atmosphere is very thin, but it is very important to us. It gives us oxygen to breathe, helps keep us warm and keeps out dangerous rays from the Sun.

IONOSPHERE

MESOSPHERE

KILOMETRES

80
70
60
50
40
30
20

STRATOSPHERE

TROPOSPHERE

## atom

The smallest part of a substance that can exist. All the atoms in a chemical element are the same. But they are different from the atoms of every other element. Atoms are so tiny that a single raindrop contains millions upon millions. We can think of the atom as being like a miniature solar system. It has a central nucleus (Sun), containing several atomic particles. Around the nucleus circle a number of electrons (planets).

nucleus

electrons

orbits (paths) of electrons

**atomic energy, see nuclear energy**

## atomizer

A simple device that produces a fine spray. A scent spray is an atomizer.

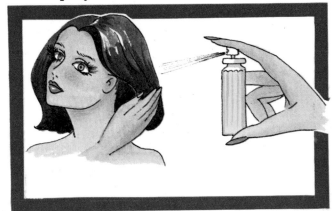

## atom smasher,
see **particle accelerator**

## aurora

A coloured glow that can be seen in the far northern and far southern skies. Often called the northern or southern lights.

## automation

The widespread use of automatic machines in industry. Only a few human operators are required in automated plants like oil refineries.

## azurite

A beautiful deep blue mineral. Its chemical name is copper carbonate.

# Bb

## balance

A pair of laboratory scales, used to weigh substances very accurately.

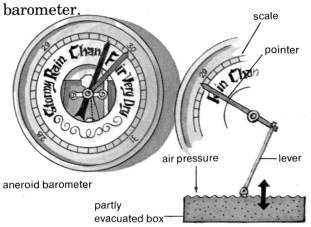

protective glass case

balance arm

weighing pans

box of weights

## barometer

An instrument that measures air pressure. The household barometer is an *aneroid* barometer.

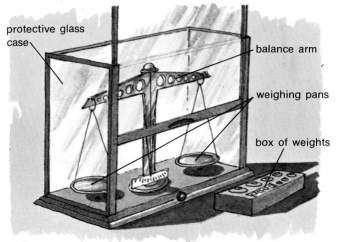

scale

pointer

air pressure

lever

aneroid barometer

partly evacuated box

## basalt

One of the two main rocks in the Earth's crust. It is dark and has small crystals.

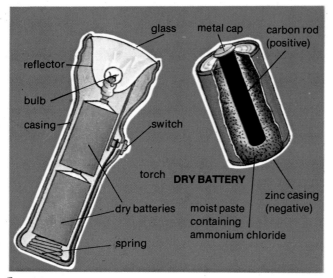

**torch** **DRY BATTERY**

## battery

A device that produces electricity by means of a chemical reaction. 'Dry' batteries are used in torches and radios. 'Wet' batteries are used in cars.

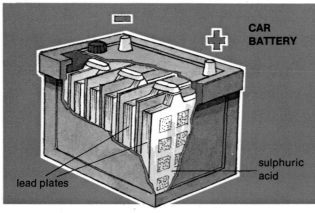

**CAR BATTERY**

## bearing

Something that supports the moving part of a machine and allows it to turn. Wheel shafts are usually held in ball bearings. Watches contain jewel bearings.

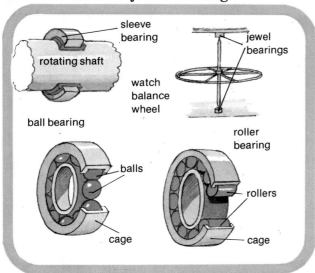

## benzene

A liquid with a sweet smell or aroma, first found in coal tar. It is one of the most important substances in chemistry. It is unusual in having its atoms arranged in the form of a ring. It is the starting point for whole families of ring compounds, most of which are strongly smelling, or aromatic.

## binoculars

A kind of twin-barrelled telescope. It is short because it contains prisms which 'fold' the light path.

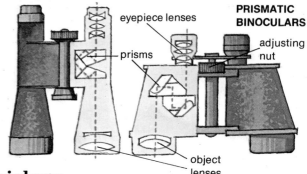

**PRISMATIC BINOCULARS**

## biology

The study of living things.

## black hole

A mysterious heavenly body that swallows up everything nearby, including light. Black holes are thought to be the remains of a large star that has collapsed.

## boiling

The condition when a liquid bubbles and changes into a gas. All liquids boil at different temperatures. The boiling point of water is 100°C; that of alcohol is 78°C.

## botany

The study of plant life.

## bunsen burner

The standard gas burner used in most laboratories, named after Robert Bunsen.

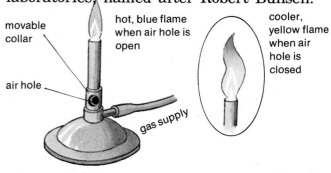

# Cc

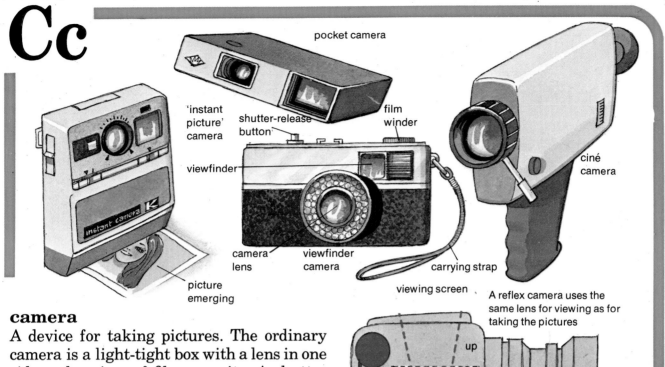

pocket camera

'instant picture' camera

shutter-release button

film winder

viewfinder

camera lens

viewfinder camera

carrying strap

ciné camera

picture emerging

viewing screen

A reflex camera uses the same lens for viewing as for taking the pictures

up

film

mirror

down

light path

lenses

## camera

A device for taking pictures. The ordinary camera is a light-tight box with a lens in one side and a piece of film opposite. A shutter allows light through the lens. The film records the light pattern falling on it. A movie camera takes a series of still photographs in quick succession. A television camera records a picture by means of electric charges.

## carbohydrate

An important group of compounds containing carbon, hydrogen and oxygen. They are found in many foods. Sugar and starch are carbohydrates.

## carbon

A chemical element with a unique property. Its atoms can combine together in long chains to make complicated substances. All living things are made up of such carbon compounds. Carbon occurs in nature in two forms—as hard diamond and soft graphite.

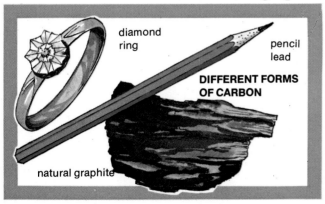

diamond ring

pencil lead

**DIFFERENT FORMS OF CARBON**

natural graphite

## carbon dioxide

The gas we breathe out, made up of carbon and oxygen. Plants take in carbon dioxide to make their food.

## catalyst

A substance that helps a chemical reaction take place, but does not itself change. The precious metal platinum is a good catalyst.

## cathode-ray tube

The part of a television receiver that changes electrical signals into pictures. The signals go to coils which make a beam of electrons (cathode-rays) scan across the screen to form a picture.

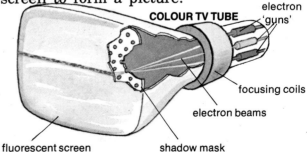

**COLOUR TV TUBE**

electron 'guns'

focusing coils

electron beams

fluorescent screen

shadow mask

## caustic soda

The common name for sodium hydroxide, the strongest alkali. It is called 'caustic' because it can burn your skin.

## cell

This is a device that produces electricity. Batteries may consist of a single cell or several cells joined together. A car battery contains six cells.

## cellulose

The substance that forms the structure of plants. It is a carbohydrate. Wood is nearly all cellulose.

## Celsius, see temperature

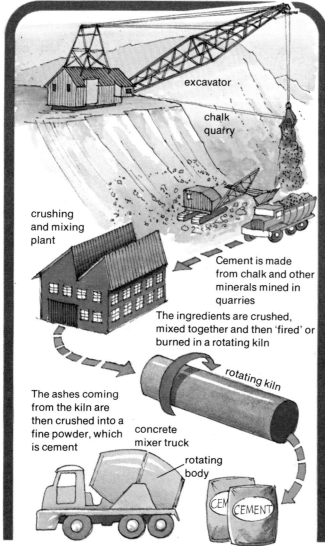

excavator

chalk quarry

crushing and mixing plant

Cement is made from chalk and other minerals mined in quarries

The ingredients are crushed, mixed together and then 'fired' or burned in a rotating kiln

rotating kiln

The ashes coming from the kiln are then crushed into a fine powder, which is cement

concrete mixer truck

rotating body

CEMENT

## cement

A grey powder which is mixed with sand, gravel and water to make concrete. A chemical reaction occurs as concrete sets.

## centigrade, see temperature

## centrifugal force

A force that acts on something travelling round in a circle. It acts outwards and balances a force that acts inwards, called the centripetal force.

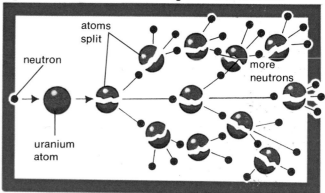

centrifugal force

## chain reaction

The reaction behind nuclear energy. Atoms of uranium split and release particles that split other atoms in rapid succession.

atoms split

neutron

more neutrons

uranium atom

## chalk

One of the commonest rocks. It is pure white and made up of a single mineral, calcium carbonate. Most chalk consists of fossils.

chalk fossils

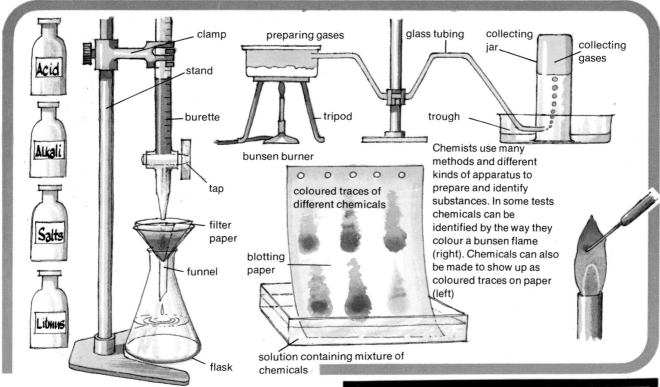

clamp
preparing gases
glass tubing
collecting jar
collecting gases
stand
burette
tap
filter paper
funnel
flask
bunsen burner
tripod
trough
coloured traces of different chemicals
blotting paper
solution containing mixture of chemicals

Chemists use many methods and different kinds of apparatus to prepare and identify substances. In some tests chemicals can be identified by the way they colour a bunsen flame (right). Chemicals can also be made to show up as coloured traces on paper (left)

Acid
Alkali
Salts
Litmus

## chemistry
The science that studies the make-up and properties of matter. It grew up from the ancient practice of alchemy. The two major branches of chemistry are *organic* chemistry, the study of carbon compounds; and *inorganic* chemistry, the study of everything else. Analytical chemistry seeks to analyse compounds—find out what they are made of. Physical chemistry investigates the physical properties of substances.

## chlorine
A greenish-coloured poisonous gas with a choking smell. It is used to purify water and is found in bleaches. Its compounds, such as sodium chloride (salt), are common.

## cloud
A mass of tiny water drops or ice crystals floating in the sky. Clouds form when air containing water vapour rises and cools. The water vapour condenses, or turns into drops.

## coal
The remains, or fossils, of giant trees and ferns that grew on Earth hundreds of millions of years ago. It consists mainly of carbon. When coal is heated strongly out of air, it forms valuable fuel gas. What remains is called coal tar.

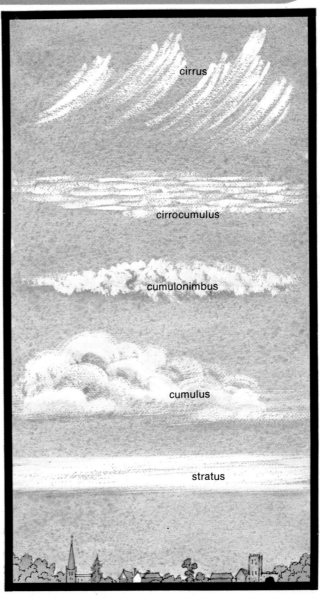

cirrus
cirrocumulus
cumulonimbus
cumulus
stratus

## colour

A property of a substance which depends on the way it behaves when light falls on it. Ordinary white light is actually a mixture of light of different colours—the colours of the spectrum. An object appears red, say, because it reflects red light but absorbs light of other colours. Any colour can be produced by mixing together light or paint of three *primary* colours.

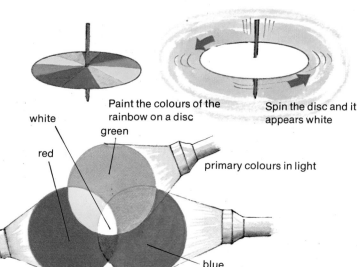

Paint the colours of the rainbow on a disc

Spin the disc and it appears white

white
green
red
primary colours in light
blue

primary colours in light

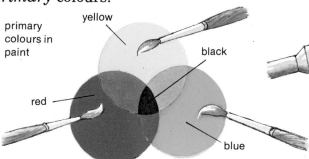

primary colours in paint
yellow
black
red
blue

## combustion

Burning. What happens when something combines with oxygen and gives out heat and light.

## comet

A heavenly body that circles around the Sun. It is a glowing mass of frozen gas and dust. Some comets have a tail, which always points away from the Sun. The most famous comet is Halley's comet, last seen in 1910.

## compass

An instrument for finding direction. It has a magnetised needle which always lines itself up in a north-south direction. This is the direction of the Earth's magnetic field.

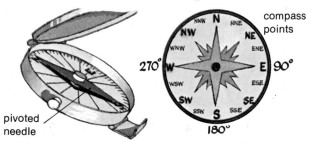

pivoted needle

compass points

270° W    E 90°

180°

## compound

What results when one chemical element joins with another. Sodium and chlorine, for example, join together to form the compound sodium chloride, or common salt.

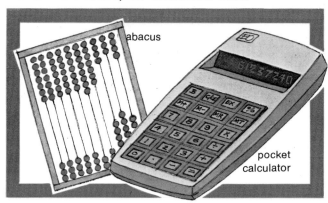

abacus

pocket calculator

## computer

A calculator, especially an electronic machine which can operate rapidly. An abacus is a simple computer; so is a pocket calculator.

## condensation

What takes place when a vapour cools and changes back into a liquid.

## conduction

A way in which heat and electricity can travel. Heat is conducted in solids when energy passes from molecule to molecule. In electrical conduction electrons carry the electricity. Metals are good conductors of heat and electricity.

## conservation

Preserving our natural resources.

## constellation

A pattern of bright stars. Ancient astronomers named the constellations after animals, heroes and other things which they thought the patterns looked like.

## convection

The way in which heat travels in a liquid or a gas. When air, for example, is heated, it expands. It therefore becomes lighter and rises, in a convection current.

Sea breezes are often caused by convection currents. On a sunny day the land heats up more than the sea, and the air above it rises. Air moves in from the sea to take its place, causing a breeze

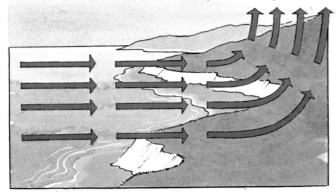

## copper

One of the oldest known metals of attractive reddish-orange colour. It can be found as a metal in the ground. It conducts heat and electricity well and does not easily corrode. It is widely used in alloys.

## corrosion

The destruction of metals under chemical attack. Iron corrodes in moist air and changes into rust. Some metals, including copper and tin, resist corrosion.

## cosmic rays

Atomic particles from outer space which strike the Earth.

## cosmonaut

The Russian term for a space traveller.

## cosmos

All that exists in space; the universe.

## cracking

Breaking down heavy molecules into lighter ones. It is an important process in refining petroleum, or crude oil.

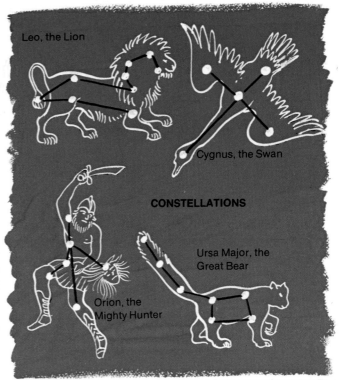

Leo, the Lion

Cygnus, the Swan

**CONSTELLATIONS**

Orion, the Mighty Hunter

Ursa Major, the Great Bear

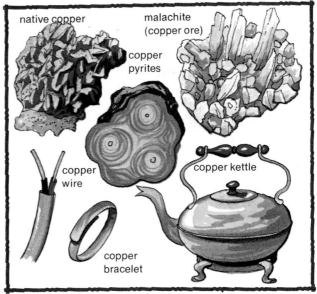

native copper

malachite (copper ore)

copper pyrites

copper wire

copper kettle

copper bracelet

Cosmonaut Yuri Gagarin became the first man to travel in Space, on 12 April 1961. He made one orbit of the Earth in a Vostok spacecraft

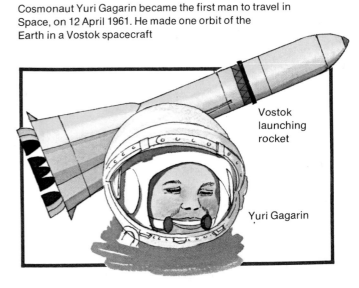

Vostok launching rocket

Yuri Gagarin

**crust**

The top layer of the Earth.

**crystals**

The beautiful shapes minerals and other substances grow into when they become solid. Sugar, for example, grows into tiny cubes when it crystallizes; so does common salt. Epsom salts grows into long needles. Each substance always crystallizes into the same shape. The finest crystals are used as gems.

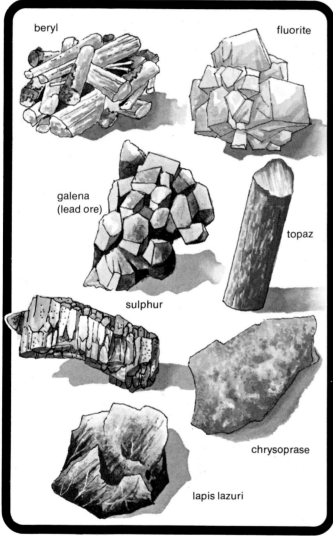

beryl

fluorite

galena (lead ore)

topaz

sulphur

chrysoprase

lapis lazuri

**cyanide**

A substance that is a deadly poison, causing instant death if swallowed.

**cycle**

A string of events that is constantly repeated. The Moon goes through its phases in a cycle of $29\frac{1}{2}$ days. A petrol engine goes through a cycle of four piston movements (strokes) to produce power.

# Dd

**day**

The time it takes the Earth to spin once on its axis in space. For telling the time we divide the day into 24 hours, or two periods of 12 hours. It is daylight, or 'day', in that part of the world facing the Sun, and night in that part in the Sun's shadow. Because the Earth's axis is tilted, there are more daylight hours in the summer than in the winter.

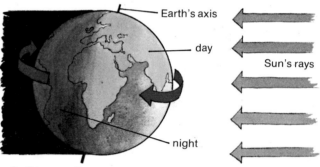

Earth's axis

day

Sun's rays

night

**delta wing**

An aircraft wing made in the shape of the Greek letter capital delta, Δ.

Concorde is a delta winged aircraft

**density**

A measure of how light or heavy a substance is. It is expressed as the weight of a unit volume of the substance. One cubic centimetre of water weighs 1 gram—its density is 1. The density of other substances is usually expressed as so many times the density of water. This is called its relative density, or specific gravity. The metal osmium has the highest relative density.

**detergent**

A cleaning agent made from petroleum chemicals which has a stronger action than soap and does not form scum.

## diamond

The hardest of all minerals, prized as a gem for its beauty. It is a form of carbon.

## diesel engine

An engine that runs on light oil, named after its inventor Rudolf Diesel. Power is produced in the engine by exploding the oil in hot, compressed air.

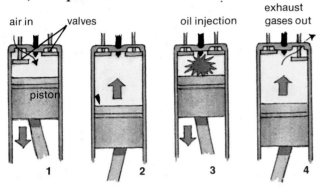

The four 'strokes' of the diesel engine cycle: (1) intake (2) compression (3) power (4) exhaust

## distillation

Boiling a liquid to produce a vapour, and then cooling the vapour so that it condenses, or changes back into liquid. It is a means of producing pure liquids.

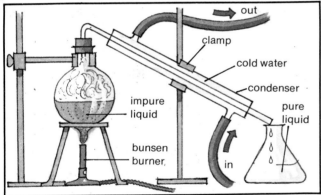

## diving bell

A chamber rather like a bell in which men can work in the dry under water.

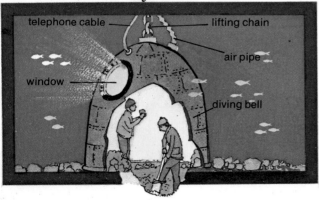

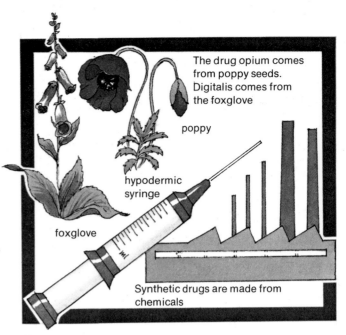

The drug opium comes from poppy seeds. Digitalis comes from the foxglove

poppy

hypodermic syringe

foxglove

Synthetic drugs are made from chemicals

## drug

A substance used to prevent and treat illness and disease. Some drugs are obtained from plants and animals; others are made from chemicals. For example, aspirin is produced from coal tar, penicillin from the penicillium mould (a plant organism).

## dry ice

Frozen carbon dioxide. It changes straight from solid into gas when it heats up, without becoming liquid first.

## dye

A substance used to colour materials. Some dyes come from plants and insects, but most are now man-made.

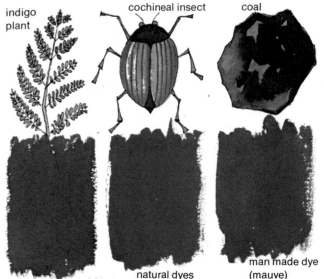

indigo plant

cochineal insect

coal

natural dyes

man made dye (mauve)

## dynamite

A powerful explosive made of nitroglycerine absorbed in a chalky earth.

# Ee

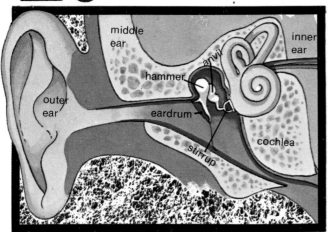

## ear

The body organ which enables us to hear and keep our balance. We can think of it as a kind of telephone. The *outer ear* collects sound waves in the air and directs them on to the ear drum. The drum vibrates, and the vibrations are passed on to delicate bones in the *middle ear* and to a fluid in the *inner ear*, which sends messages to the brain.

## Earth

The planet on which we live. Like all planets it circles around the Sun (once a year) and spins on its axis like a top (once a day) while it does so. It is the only planet in our solar system that is not too hot and not too cold to support life.

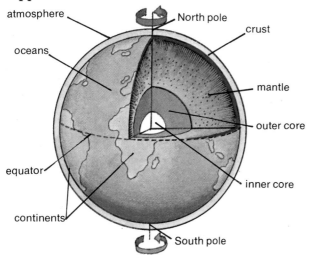

The Earth is the third planet out from the Sun, after Mercury and Venus. It is a near-circular ball of rock with a diameter of some 12,756 km at the equator.

## earthquake

Violent shaking of the ground. Earthquakes occur when parts of the Earth's crust that have been locked together suddenly move.

## echo

Sound that has been reflected from an object back into our ears.

## echo location, see radar, sonar

## eclipse

What happens when one heavenly body passes in front of another and blots out its light. An eclipse of the Sun occurs when the Moon passes in front of the Sun. An eclipse of the Moon occurs when the Moon passes into the Earth's shadow.

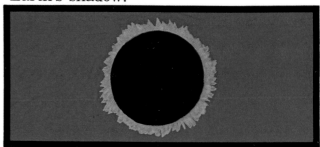

## electric arc

A dazzling flame produced when electricity jumps between two points.

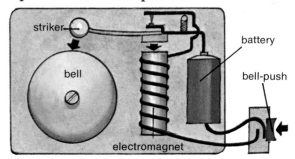

## electric bell

The usual kind of door bell. When the bell push is pressed, current from a battery flows to an electromagnet which pulls the striker on to the bell.

## electric charge

Electrons have a kind of electricity we call negative. We say they have a negative electric charge. Atoms may gain electrons and acquire a negative charge. Atoms may lose electrons and acquire an opposite kind of electricity, which we call a positive charge.

## electric circuit

A path along which an electric current flows. A simple circuit includes a battery to produce the current, the device which the battery operates, and wire to link them together.

## electric current

A flow of electricity from a battery or generator. It may flow in one direction only (direct current, DC) or it may flow first one way, then the other (alternating current, AC).

## electric generator

A machine that produces, or generates electricity. It works because electricity is produced in a coil of wire when it is spun in a magnetic field.

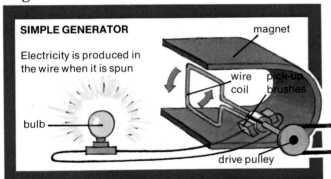

SIMPLE GENERATOR

Electricity is produced in the wire when it is spun

bulb
magnet
wire coil
pick-up brushes
drive pulley

## electricity

A basic property of matter which we can use to provide energy. The electricity we use in the home is *current* electricity. It is a flow of electrons. The other type of electricity is *static* electricity. It exists between things which have an electric charge.

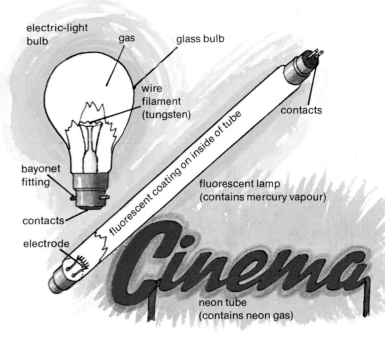

electric-light bulb
gas
glass bulb
wire filament (tungsten)
contacts
bayonet fitting
contacts
electrode
fluorescent coating on inside of tube
fluorescent lamp (contains mercury vapour)
Cinema
neon tube (contains neon gas)

## electric light

Light given off when electricity heats a thin wire (filament) to white heat, or when it passes through certain gases.

## electric motor

A machine that is driven by electricity. It works because a coil in a magnetic field spins when electricity is passed through it. It is built in much the same way as a generator.

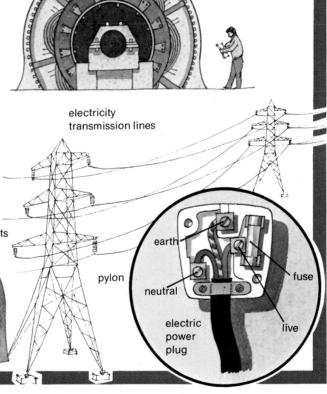

electricity generator

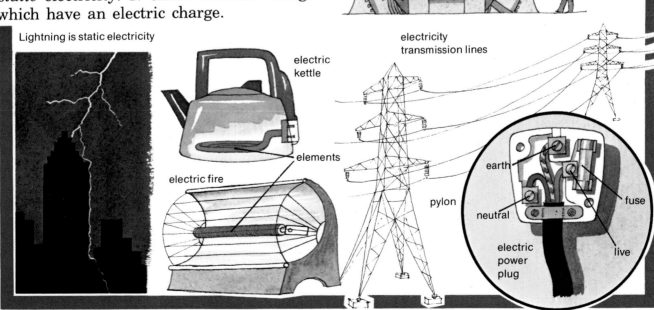

Lightning is static electricity
electric kettle
elements
electric fire
electricity transmission lines
pylon
earth
neutral
fuse
live
electric power plug

## electrolysis

Splitting up a chemical compound by means of electricity. Water can be split up by electrolysis into its elements—hydrogen and oxygen.

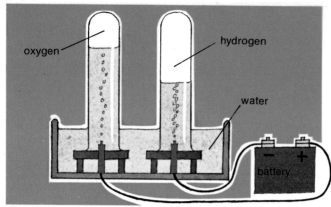

## electromagnet

A device which becomes a magnet when electricity is passed through it. It is made up of coils of wire wound around an iron core.

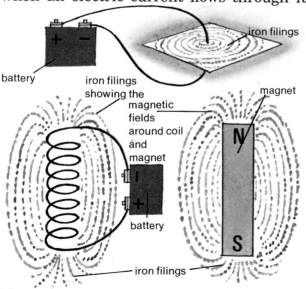

## electromagnetism

Study of the connection between electricity and magnetism. It starts with the fact that a magnetic field is produced around a wire when an electric current flows through it.

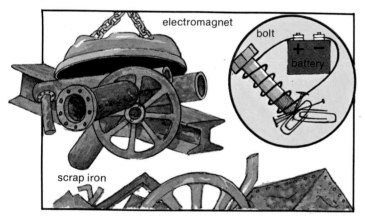

## electron

A tiny particle with an electric charge which is present in all atoms. Electrons circle around the nucleus of an atom like planets around the Sun.

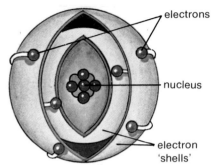

Oxygen has six electrons circling around the nucleus. They circle at different distances in so-called 'shells'

## electronics

The branch of science that makes possible such things as radio and television, computers and radar. It deals with the flow of electrons (electric current) through a vacuum, through gases, and through transistors and other semi-conductors.

## electroplating

Coating one metal with another by means of electricity. Cheap metals like steel are often plated with metals like chromium to make them look more attractive and prevent them rusting.

## electrostatics, see static electricity

## element, chemical

One of the basic 'building blocks' from which all matter is made up. Some elements are gases, a few are liquids, but most are solids. Everything about us is made up of one or more chemical elements combined together. Ninety-two elements are found in nature. A further 14 elements have been made artificially by bombarding natural elements with atomic particles. The table opposite gives the names of the elements. They are numbered in order from the simplest to the most complex. The number also equals the number of protons and electrons in their atoms.

## emulsion

A mixture of small droplets of one liquid in another. Milk is an emulsion consisting of small fat droplets in a watery solution.

## energy

Ability to do work. Heat, light and electricity are different forms of energy. Most of the energy we use on Earth came originally from the Sun. Our bodies use food made by plants to give us energy. Plants use the Sun's energy to make food. The Sun's energy is stored in fuels such as oil, coal and natural gas. A moving object has *kinetic energy*. An object at rest can have *potential energy*. A ball on a table has potential energy. This is released when the ball falls.

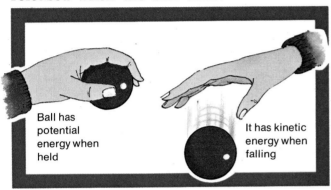

Ball has potential energy when held

It has kinetic energy when falling

## engine

A machine that harnesses energy to do useful work. A petrol engine uses the energy stored in petrol to move the wheels of a car. A steam turbine uses the energy in steam to spin a ship's propeller. They are both *heat engines*, which change heat into work.

## Equator

An imaginary line drawn around the widest part of the Earth, midway between the poles.

Equator

## equinox

Time of the year when day and night are of equal length. The spring (vernal) equinox is on about 21 March. The autumnal equinox is on about 23 September.

## erosion

Wearing away of the Earth's land surface by natural forces, such as flowing water, ocean waves, moving glaciers and blowing sand. Erosion helped by the action of rain, wind, Sun and frost is called *weathering*.

wind and rain

running water

**AGENTS OF EROSION**

waves

frost and ice

## evaporation

The change of a liquid into a vapour (gas). Liquids evaporate more quickly as they approach boiling point.

| The Chemical Elements | | | | | |
|---|---|---|---|---|---|
| 1 Hydrogen | 19 Potassium | 37 Rubidium | 55 Caesium | 73 Tantalum | 91 Protactinium |
| 2 Helium | 20 Calcium | 38 Strontium | 56 Barium | 74 Tungsten | 92 Uranium |
| 3 Lithium | 21 Scandium | 39 Yttrium | 57 Lanthanum | 75 Rhenium | 93 Neptunium |
| 4 Beryllium | 22 Titanium | 40 Zirconium | 58 Cerium | 76 Osmium | 94 Plutonium |
| 5 Boron | 23 Vanadium | 41 Niobium | 59 Praseodymium | 77 Iridium | 95 Americium |
| 6 Carbon | 24 Chromium | 42 Molybdenum | 60 Neodymium | 78 Platinum | 96 Curium |
| 7 Nitrogen | 25 Manganese | 43 Technetium | 61 Promethium | 79 Gold | 97 Berkelium |
| 8 Oxygen | 26 Iron | 44 Ruthenium | 62 Samarium | 80 Mercury | 98 Californium |
| 9 Fluorine | 27 Cobalt | 45 Rhodium | 63 Europium | 81 Thallium | 99 Einsteinium |
| 10 Neon | 28 Nickel | 46 Palladium | 64 Gadolinium | 82 Lead | 100 Fermium |
| 11 Sodium | 29 Copper | 47 Silver | 65 Terbium | 83 Bismuth | 101 Mendelevium |
| 12 Magnesium | 30 Zinc | 48 Cadmium | 66 Dysprosium | 84 Polonium | 102 Nobelium |
| 13 Aluminium | 31 Gallium | 49 Indium | 67 Holmium | 85 Astatine | 103 Lawrencium |
| 14 Silicon | 32 Germanium | 50 Tin | 68 Erbium | 86 Radon | 104 Rutherfordium |
| 15 Phosphorus | 33 Arsenic | 51 Antimony | 69 Thulium | 87 Francium | 105 Hahnium |
| 16 Sulphur | 34 Selenium | 52 Tellurium | 70 Ytterbium | 88 Radium | 106 Unnamed |
| 17 Chlorine | 35 Bromine | 53 Iodine | 71 Lutetium | 89 Actinium | |
| 18 Argon | 36 Krypton | 54 Xenon | 72 Hafnium | 90 Thorium | |

## eye

The body organ which enables us to see. It works much like a camera. It is a liquid-filled ball with a lens in the front and a screen (retina) at the back. The lens focuses light into an image on the retina, which sends messages to the brain through the optic nerve.

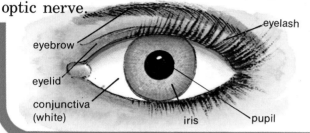

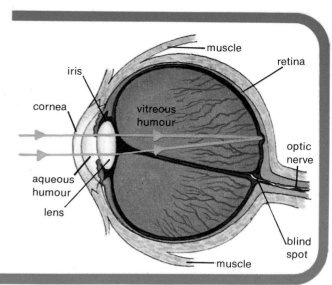

# Ff

**Fahrenheit,** see **temperature**

## fall-out

Dust and other material that falls from the sky after a nuclear-bomb explosion. It is dangerous because it is radioactive.

## fat

One of the most important foods of animals, which provides them with much of their energy. Animals store the fat they do not use in their body tissues. Common fats include suet (beef fat), lard (pig fat), butter (milk fat) and fish and plant oils.

## fault

A break in the rock layers caused by movements of the Earth's crust. Valleys may be formed when a block of crust slips. They are called rift valleys. The most famous is the Great Rift Valley in East Africa.

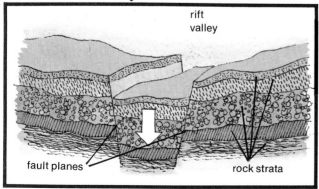

## fermentation

The process in which yeast changes plant sugars into alcohol. Wine (from grapes), cider (from apples) and beer (from barley) are alcoholic drinks made by fermentation. Carbon dioxide gas is also produced in fermentation, which explains why beer and cider are slightly 'gassy'.

## film

The material in a camera which receives the light image. Ordinary film consists of a long plastic strip wound into a roll. The strip is coated with silver salts, which change when light falls on them. In developing, chemicals are added to make these changes visible. Colour film is made up of several layers which record light of different colours. The images in each layer are dyed to produce a colour picture.

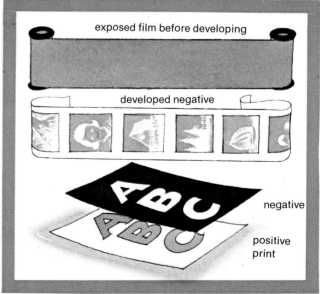

## fire

The heat and light produced when substances burn. Under control it is one of man's best friends. Out of control it is one of his worst enemies.

fire—friend . . .

. . . and foe

## fission

The splitting of an atom, or rather the nucleus of an atom. When fission occurs, great amounts of energy are given out. Uranium is one metal whose atoms split quite easily. We use uranium as a 'fuel' in nuclear reactors.

## fog

A cloud that forms near the ground. A *smog* is a choking fog which forms in polluted air in many industrial cities.

## force

In the simplest sense, a push or a pull which tries to make something move, or slow down, or change direction. Gravity is a force that attracts. Magnetism is a force that can both attract and repel.

## forging

Shaping metal by first heating it and then hammering it. Forging is done in industry by huge drop hammers and powerful forging presses.

drop forging

hammer forging

## fossil

The remains or impression of plants or animals that once lived on Earth. They may be found in rocks, in ice and in amber. Studying fossils is called *paleontology*.

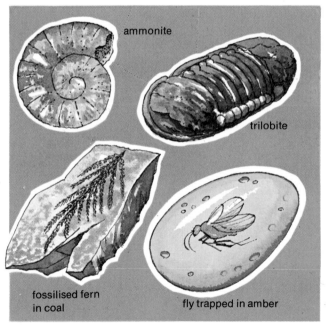

ammonite

trilobite

fossilised fern in coal

fly trapped in amber

## freezing

What happens when a liquid changes into a solid as it is cooled. Every liquid freezes at a certain temperature, called the freezing point. Water freezes at 0°C; but alcohol does not freeze until −117°C. Water is unusual because it expands, or increases in size, when it freezes into ice.

## friction

The resistance that tries to prevent one object moving against another. You have to overcome friction before you can push a book across a table top, for example. There is greater friction between rough objects than between smooth objects. Whenever friction occurs, heat is produced.

Friction provides the energy to set a match alight

frosty patterns on window panes

## frost

Feathery ice crystals that form on plants and window panes when water vapour comes out of the air and freezes.

## furnace

A structure in which fuel is burned to produce heat. Home central heating systems have small furnaces to heat the water that passes through the radiators. Industrial furnaces are huge and are used for smelting and refining metals.

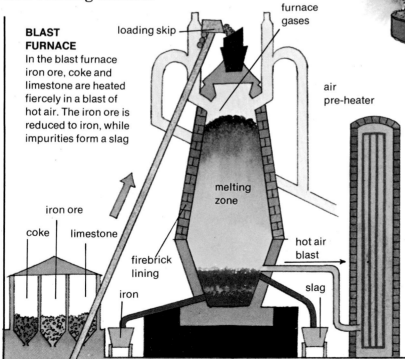

**BLAST FURNACE**
In the blast furnace iron ore, coke and limestone are heated fiercely in a blast of hot air. The iron ore is reduced to iron, while impurities form a slag

loading skip
furnace gases
air pre-heater
melting zone
coke
iron ore
limestone
firebrick lining
iron
hot air blast
slag

## fuse

A wire that is the 'weak link' in an electric circuit. When too much current passes through it, it melts and breaks the circuit. It protects other electrical devices in the circuit.

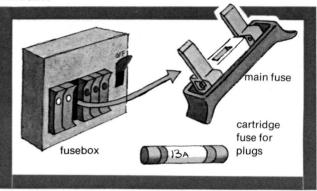

main fuse
cartridge fuse for plugs
fusebox
13A

## fusion

The combining together of light atoms to form heavier ones. When this takes place, large amounts of energy are given out. Fusion reactions take place in the Sun and produce all its energy. In these reactions atoms of hydrogen combine together to form helium atoms. A similar reaction occurs in hydrogen bombs.

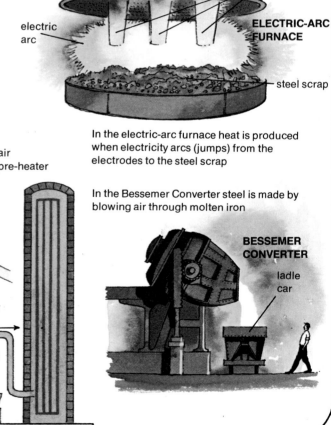

red-hot electrodes
electric arc
**ELECTRIC-ARC FURNACE**
steel scrap

In the electric-arc furnace heat is produced when electricity arcs (jumps) from the electrodes to the steel scrap

In the Bessemer Converter steel is made by blowing air through molten iron

**BESSEMER CONVERTER**
ladle car

# Gg

## galaxy

A star family, or system in space. The galaxy to which our Sun belongs contains about 100,000 million stars. We call it the Milky Way. Like many galaxies in space, our galaxy has a spiral shape. Other galaxies are oval, or elliptical in shape.

## galena

The main ore of lead, which has attractive crystals. It often contains traces of silver. Another name for it is lead glance.

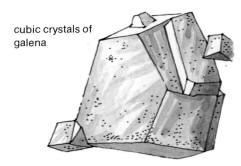

cubic crystals of galena

## galvanizing

Coating with zinc. Iron and steel are galvanized so that they do not rust.

## gamma-rays

Invisible rays given out by radioactive substances. They are penetrating and lethal.

## gas

One of the three main forms, or states of matter. The others are solid and liquid. Gases, such as air, are lighter than solids and liquids. Their molecules are much farther apart. Gases have no shape but take the shape of any container they are put in.

Carbon dioxide is the fizzy gas in drinks

Hydrogen sulphide is the smelly gas in bad eggs

Hydrogen is the very light gas in balloons

Methane is the main gas in cooking gas

## gas turbine

An engine in which a turbine wheel is spun by a stream of hot gas. The jet engine is one form of gas turbine.

## gauge

An instrument used to measure such things as pressure, thickness and temperature.

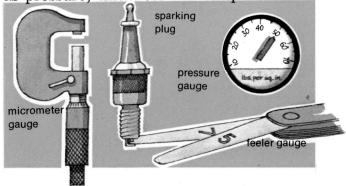

sparking plug

pressure gauge

lbs. per sq. in.

micrometer gauge

feeler gauge

## gems

Beautiful minerals, stones and other materials which are used in jewellery. Many are very hard crystals which are cut to show great brilliance.

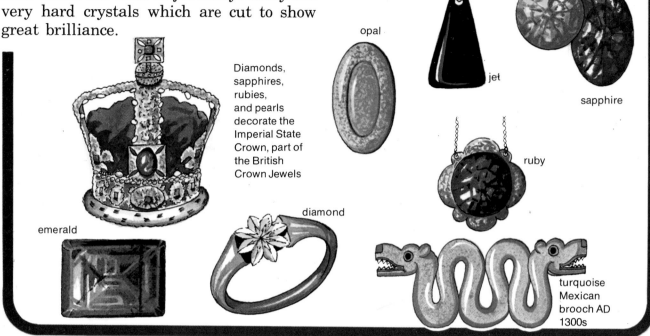

Diamonds, sapphires, rubies, and pearls decorate the Imperial State Crown, part of the British Crown Jewels

opal

jet

sapphire

ruby

emerald

diamond

turquoise Mexican brooch AD 1300s

## geography

Study of the Earth's surface, its climate, and the places and peoples that exist on it.

## geology

Study of the Earth's crust, and the changes that take place in it. Geologists study rocks and minerals and mountain-forming, together with earthquakes and fossils.

## geyser

A spring that blows out fountains of steam and hot water from time to time. Most famous is 'Old Faithful' in Yellowstone National Park in the United States.

## glacier

A slowly moving 'river' of ice. Glaciers are found in high mountainous regions in many parts of the world. During the Ice Ages glaciers caused a great deal of erosion, creating deep valleys.

## glass

One of our most useful materials, made mainly from sand. It is valuable because it is transparent; it is not affected by most chemicals; and it can be shaped easily. Ordinary glass is made by heating sand with limestone and soda in a furnace. Heat-proof 'oven' glass contains other ingredients. Glass is not a crystal, as you might think, but a supercooled liquid.

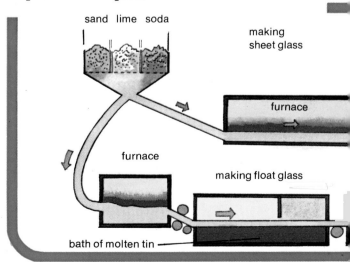

sand lime soda

making sheet glass

furnace

furnace

making float glass

bath of molten tin

## gold

A rare, precious and heavy metal of attractive yellow colour, which can be found as a metal in the ground. It is quite soft but does not corrode.

native gold

gold ring

gold bullion

hallmark

## granite

One of the commonest rocks in the Earth's crust. It contains the minerals feldspar, mica and quartz.

## graphite

A black mineral form of carbon used in pencil 'lead'. It is one of the softest minerals.

## gravity

The 'pull' of the Earth, or the force the Earth exerts on any object on it or near it in space. All the heavenly bodies exert a similar kind of pull. The Moon's gravity causes the tides.

## gyroscope

A spinning device which can perform balancing tricks.

# Hh

## heat

A form of energy, which is related to the movement of molecules. It is the kinetic energy possessed by the molecules of a substance. A substance is hotter when its molecules move faster. Many areas of science are concerned with the effects of heat on substances. Most materials expand, or increase in size, when they are heated. By adding heat to, or taking heat from, a substance, you can make it change its state.

## heat shield

A plastic coating on a spacecraft which prevents it from overheating when it returns to Earth. The heat is produced by friction of the spacecraft with the air.

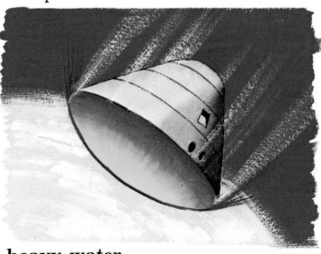

## heavy water

Water containing a heavier form of hydrogen, called deuterium. It is used in some atomic reactors.

drawing chamber

glass sheets

glass blowing

glass sheets

heat-proof glass

cut glass

fibreglass

engraved glass

stained glass

## holography
A way of producing life-like, three-dimensional photographs using laser beams.

## hovercraft
A craft that glides along on a 'cushion' of air. The cushion is produced by a downward-facing fan. Hovercraft are propelled by air propellers.

## humidity
The amount of moisture, or water vapour in the air. When the air is very humid, our bodies feel 'sticky' because our skin cannot get rid of perspiration.

## hurricane
A very powerful storm in which winds can blow at speeds of more than 150 kilometres an hour. Strictly speaking, hurricanes are violent storms that form in the Caribbean Sea. Similar storms in the Indian and Pacific Oceans are called *cyclones* or *typhoons*.

## hydraulics
A branch of science concerned with the flow of liquids. Hydraulic machines, such as car brakes, work by means of liquid pressure.

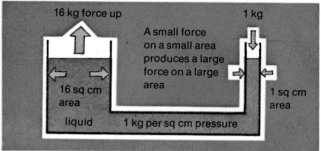

16 kg force up — 1 kg
A small force on a small area produces a large force on a large area
16 sq cm area — 1 sq cm area
liquid — 1 kg per sq cm pressure

## hydrocarbon
A substance containing hydrogen and carbon only. Oil is a mixture of hydrocarbons.

## hydrochloric acid
A powerful acid composed of hydrogen and chlorine. It forms salts called chlorides.

## hydrofoil
An underwater 'wing' fitted to some boats which lifts the hull out of the water.

hydrofoils

## hydrogen
The lightest of all gases. Its name means 'water-former', and it occurs with oxygen in water ($H_2O$). It burns readily and is a good fuel.

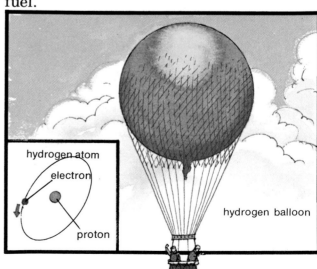

hydrogen atom
electron
proton
hydrogen balloon

# Ii

## ice
Water frozen solid. Water is unusual because it expands, or gets bigger, when it freezes. Ice is, therefore, lighter than water and floats on it. Great ice sheets cover the North and South Poles of the Earth. They break up at the edges to form huge icebergs.

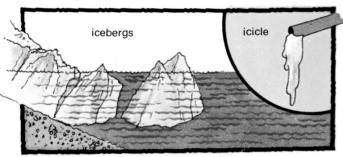

## igneous rock, see rocks

## inert gas
A rare gas which does not usually combine chemically with other elements. There are six inert gases—helium, neon, argon, krypton, xenon and radon.

## inertia
The property every object has of resisting a change in its motion. The heavier an object is, the greater is its inertia.

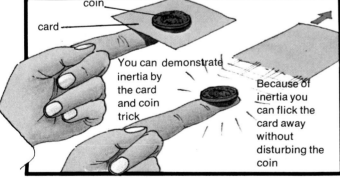

You can demonstrate inertia by the card and coin trick

Because of inertia you can flick the card away without disturbing the coin

## infra-red rays
Heat rays, which we can feel but not see.

## inorganic
Something non-living. Inorganic chemistry is the study of all the chemical elements with the exception of carbon. The study of carbon compounds is called *organic chemistry.*

## insecticide
A substance which kills insects. Pyrethrum is a natural insecticide obtained from certain daisies. DDT (dichloro-diphenyl-trichloroethane) is a man-made insecticide. Like many man-made insecticides it has dangerous long-term effects on living things.

## insulation
Something that offers protection against heat or cold, electricity or sound.

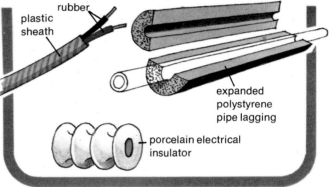

## iodine
A useful chemical element related to chlorine. It is a soft solid, which forms a purple vapour. In solution it is widely used as an antiseptic.

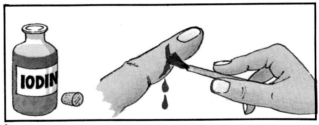

## ion
An atom which has lost or gained one or more electrons. Ions carry electric current in solutions.

## iron
One of the most important metals, valuable because it can be made into steel. It is obtained by smelting iron ore with coke in a blast furnace. Another valuable property of iron is that it is magnetic.

## isotope
The atoms in an element are not always identical. They all contain the same number of protons. But they may contain a different number of neutrons. Such atoms are called isotopes.

# Jj

## jet engine

An aircraft engine which burns fuel to produce a stream, or jet of gases. The jet propels the aircraft. The simplest jet engine is the *turbo-jet.* In a *turbo-prop* engine the jet stream drives a propeller. A more economical engine is the turbo-fan, which has a huge fan in front.

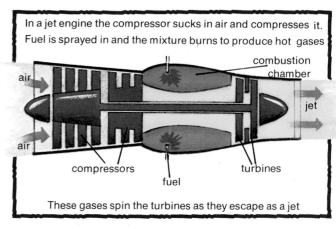

In a jet engine the compressor sucks in air and compresses it. Fuel is sprayed in and the mixture burns to produce hot gases

air · air · compressors · fuel · combustion chamber · turbines · jet

These gases spin the turbines as they escape as a jet

RB-211 TURBOFAN

fan · turbines · compressor · exhaust

## jet propulsion

The principle on which jet and rocket engines work. These engines burn fuel to produce hot gases. As the gases shoot backwards as a jet, the engine is thrust forwards by reaction.

## Jupiter

The largest of the planets, with a diameter of 143,000 km—11 times that of Earth. It consists mainly of gaseous and liquid hydrogen. It has a great red spot on its surface, and has at least 15 moons.

# Kk

## kite

The earliest flying device, dating back to about 300 BC. It lifts itself into the air in much the same way as an aerofoil, or aeroplane wing. It is usually made of a light frame covered with paper or cloth. The Chinese are famous for their kites.

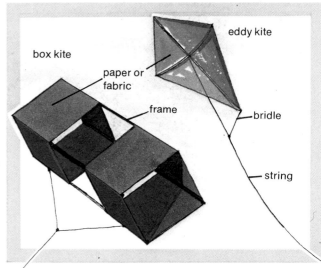

box kite · eddy kite · paper or fabric · frame · bridle · string

# Ll

## laboratory
A place where scientists carry out experiments.

## laser
A device which produces a very pure and intense beam of light. Some laser beams are powerful enough to cut metal. Unlike an ordinary light beam a laser beam does not spread very much. Lasers are increasingly used in industry and also in medicine.

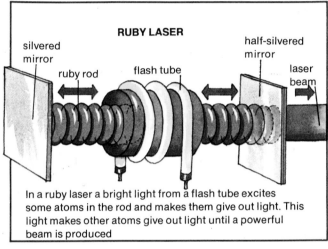

**RUBY LASER**

silvered mirror
ruby rod
flash tube
half-silvered mirror
laser beam

In a ruby laser a bright light from a flash tube excites some atoms in the rod and makes them give out light. This light makes other atoms give out light until a powerful beam is produced

## lava
The molten rock that flows from a volcano. It may cool quite slowly to form basalt rock, or very quickly to form volcanic glass (obsidian) or pumice.

pumice          obsidian

## lens
A curved piece of glass or other transparent material which bends light rays. Depending on their shape, lenses can make light rays converge or diverge.

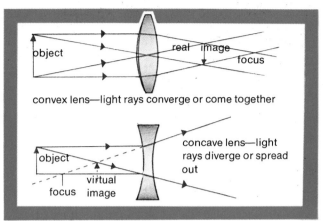

object          real image          focus

convex lens—light rays converge or come together

object

concave lens—light rays diverge or spread out

focus          virtual image

## lever
A simple machine which helps us to move a large load with a smaller effort. A crowbar and wheelbarrow are different kinds of lever. In each kind, the effort and load turn about a pivot, or fulcrum.

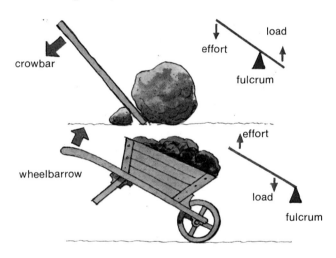

crowbar

load
effort
fulcrum

wheelbarrow

effort

load
fulcrum

## light
Rays that our eyes can detect. Light is made up of waves which are kinds of electrical and magnetic vibrations. Ordinary white sunlight is a mixture of waves of different lengths. We can see these waves as light of different colours in a spectrum or rainbow. Light travels at the incredible speed of 300,000 km per second. Nothing can travel faster. Light may come from several sources. Our daylight comes from the Sun. Artificial light comes from the heated wire in a light bulb. Laser light is a very pure light given off by excited atoms.

## lightning

A gigantic electric spark which zigzags between the clouds and the ground. The electricity it carries is millions of times stronger than the mains electricity in the home. It is a form of static electricity.

## light-year

The distance light travels in a year—about 10 million million kilometres. Astronomers use light-years as units for measuring the vast distances in space.

## lime

Material made from limestone. Quicklime is made by roasting the limestone. It is dangerous to handle because it burns flesh. Slaked lime is made by adding water to quicklime. Farmers and gardeners use it to improve their soils.

## limestone

A common rock, made up of calcium carbonate. It is quite soft and slowly dissolves in water. Limestone regions are riddled with caves and underground streams.

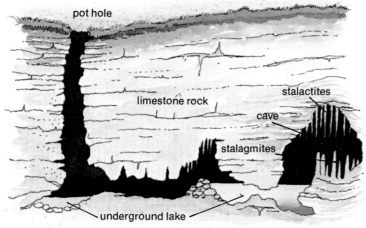

## liquid

One of the three main states of matter—the others are solid and gas. The molecules of a liquid are free to move, but not as free as in gases.

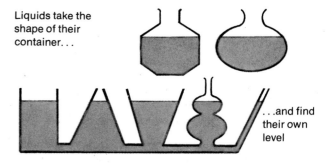

Liquids take the shape of their container. . .

. . .and find their own level

## liquid air

Air which has been cooled so that it turns into liquid. This happens at a temperature of about −193°C.

## litmus paper

Coloured paper used for testing whether something is acid or alkaline. Litmus is a dye obtained from a plant.

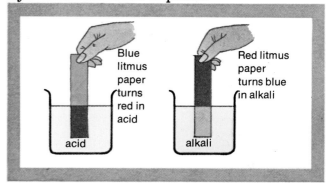

Blue litmus paper turns red in acid

Red litmus paper turns blue in alkali

acid

alkali

## loudspeaker

The device in radios, record players and the like which changes electrical signals into sound-waves.

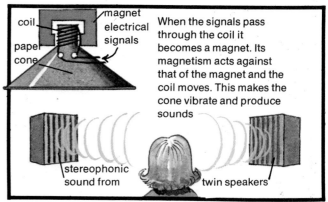

coil

magnet

electrical signals

paper cone

When the signals pass through the coil it becomes a magnet. Its magnetism acts against that of the magnet and the coil moves. This makes the cone vibrate and produce sounds

stereophonic sound from

twin speakers

## lunar

Of the Moon; from the Latin word for Moon, *luna*.

# Mm

## machine

Something that performs work. Most modern machines are very complicated. But they are in fact made up of lots of simple machines joined together. The simplest machines of all are the wheel; the inclined plane, or wedge; and the lever.

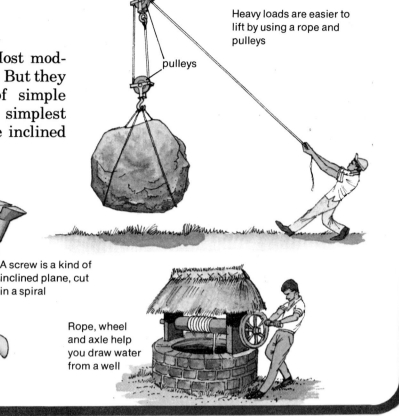

Heavy loads are easier to lift by using a rope and pulleys

pulleys

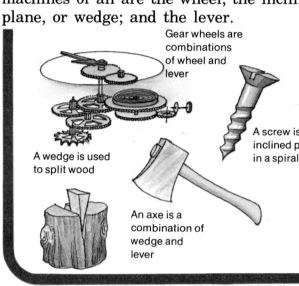

Gear wheels are combinations of wheel and lever

A wedge is used to split wood

A screw is a kind of inclined plane, cut in a spiral

An axe is a combination of wedge and lever

Rope, wheel and axle help you draw water from a well

## magma

Hot molten rock inside the Earth's crust.

## magnet

A device which can pick up objects made of iron and steel. Most magnets are themselves made of iron. In a magnet the magnetism seems to be concentrated at the ends, which are called poles. The Earth acts like a gigantic magnet with poles in the north and south.

When you suspend a magnet, one end (N) points north, the other (S) south

Unlike poles attract one another

Like poles repel one another

## magnetic field

The region around a magnet where its magnetism acts. You can see a magnetic field if you sprinkle iron filings on a card above a magnet. It appears to act in curved lines.

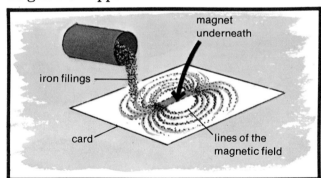

magnet underneath

iron filings

card

lines of the magnetic field

## magnifying glass

A lens which makes objects appear larger.

**mains**

The electricity that comes to our homes. In most countries mains electricity is an alternating (two-way) current of about 230 volts. This is 150 times the strength of an ordinary torch battery.

**marble**

An attractive hard rock related to limestone.

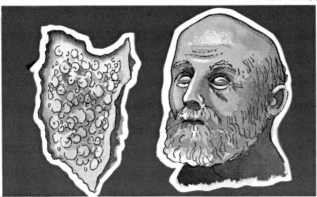

**Mars**

A small rocky planet which shines with an unmistakable red-orange colour. Its diameter is 6,790 km, a little more than half that of the Earth. It has two moons.

**mass**

The amount of matter in an object. It does not change whether that object is on the Earth, the Moon or in space. It is different from weight.

**matter**

The material—atoms and molecules—of which everything is made up.

**melting**

What happens when a solid substance turns into a liquid. Each substance melts at a fixed temperature which we call its melting point. Ice melts at 0°C; iron at about 1,500°C.

**mercury**

The only metal that is liquid at ordinary temperatures. It is called quicksilver because of the way it moves.

**Mercury**

The planet closest to the Sun. It is a ball of hot rock, 4,850 km across.

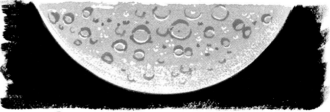

**metals**

Chemical elements which are generally hard, shiny, heavy, and silvery in colour. Only a few metals occur as metals in the ground. Most occur as compounds with other elements. Most metals are used in mixtures, or alloys, which are usually much stronger than pure metals. By far the most important metal is the alloy we call steel.

Most metals conduct heat well

Most metals are easy to shape when hot. This may be done by casting the molten metal in moulds

**metamorphic rock,** see **rocks**

## meteor

A fiery streak in the night sky. It is caused by a lump of rock or metal burning up as it passes through the atmosphere. Some lumps reach the ground, as meteorites.

a stony meteorite

This crater in Arizona was made by a meteorite which fell about 50,000 years ago. It is over 1200 metres across

## meteorology

The study of the weather.

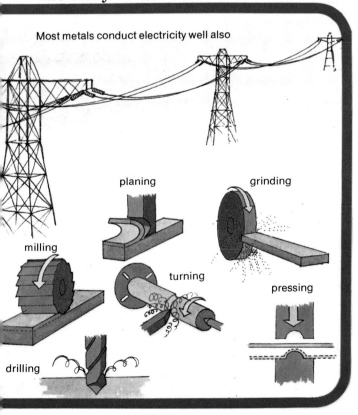

Most metals conduct electricity well also

planing

grinding

milling

turning

pressing

drilling

## microphone

A device that changes sounds into electrical signals. Microphones contain something that the sounds make vibrate. Then the vibrations are changed into electrical signals.

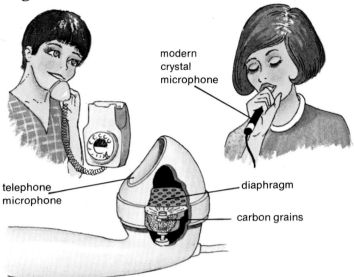

modern crystal microphone

telephone microphone

diaphragm

carbon grains

## microscope

An instrument for making tiny things appear larger. It does this by means of a number of lenses.

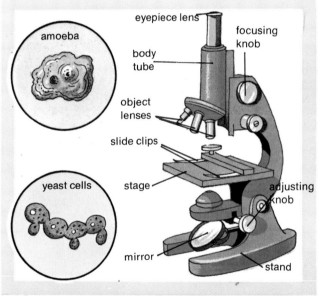

amoeba

eyepiece lens

focusing knob

body tube

object lenses

slide clips

yeast cells

stage

adjusting knob

mirror

stand

## microwaves

Very short radio waves. They are used in radar; to transmit radio and television signals; and even to cook food.

## Milky Way

A faint band of light across the night sky due to millions of distant stars. When you gaze at the Milky Way, you are looking edgeways into our galaxy.

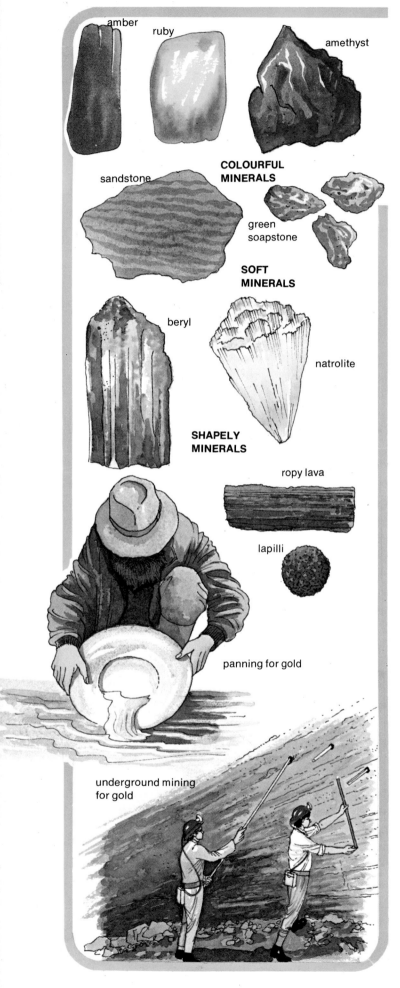

amber
ruby
amethyst

**COLOURFUL MINERALS**

sandstone

green soapstone

**SOFT MINERALS**

beryl

natrolite

**SHAPELY MINERALS**

ropy lava

lapilli

panning for gold

underground mining for gold

## minerals

The substances that make up the rocks in the Earth's crust. Among the most useful minerals are the ores, which can be made into metals. Among the most precious are the rare and beautiful minerals we know as gems. Some minerals, such as sulphur and graphite, are made up of a single chemical element. Most minerals, however, contain two or more elements combined together.

## mirage

A scene that fools your eyes. On a hot day you can often see on a road in the distance what appears to be a pool of water. But the pool is a mirage. It is a picture of the sky reflected by a layer of hot air.

## mirror

A surface that reflects light. Common mirrors are glass sheets with a thin metal coating on one side. Curved mirrors act much like lenses.

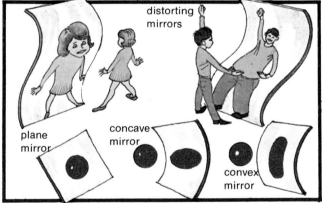

distorting mirrors

plane mirror

concave mirror

convex mirror

## molecule

A tiny particle of matter, made up of atoms linked together. Almost all matter exists as molecules and not as individual atoms.

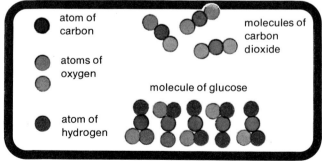

atom of carbon

molecules of carbon dioxide

atoms of oxygen

molecule of glucose

atom of hydrogen

## monsoon

A wind of the Indian Ocean which changes direction season by season. The summer monsoon is wet, the winter one dry.

## Moon

Earth's only satellite and our nearest neighbour in space. It lies about 385,000 km away, and is a solid ball of rock, 3,476 km in diameter. It is a dead world with no air, water or life of any kind. The dark regions we see on the Moon are flat areas called maria (seas). The light regions are rugged highlands covered in craters. The Apollo astronaut Neil Armstrong was the first human being to set foot on the Moon on 21 July 1969.

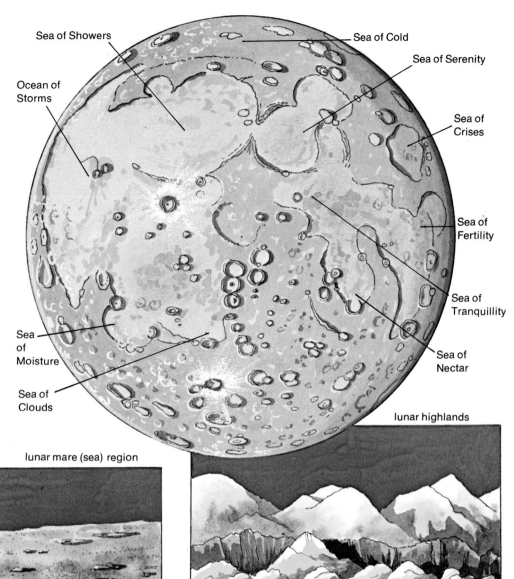

Sea of Showers
Sea of Cold
Sea of Serenity
Ocean of Storms
Sea of Crises
Sea of Fertility
Sea of Moisture
Sea of Tranquillity
Sea of Clouds
Sea of Nectar
lunar highlands
lunar mare (sea) region

# Nn

### natural gas

A mixture of gases found in the rocks, often with oil deposits. It is made up mainly of methane gas and is a very important fuel.

### nebula

A great cloud of gas and dust in space. It may appear dark or shine brightly. The one shown on the right is the Orion nebula.

### neon

A rare gas which glows a brilliant red when electricity is passed through it.

## Neptune

The eighth planet, going out from the Sun. Discovered in 1846, it has a diameter of some 50,200 km and is thought to be made up mainly of gas.

## neutralization

What happens when an alkali and an acid mix. The alkali destroys, or neutralizes, the acid, forming a salt and water.

## neutron

A tiny particle found in the nucleus of atoms. It is electrically neutral, that is, has no electric charge.

## nitric acid

One of the three most powerful acids, which strongly attacks animal and vegetable matter. It is widely used in industry to make dyes and explosives. It forms salts called nitrates.

## nitrogen

The main gas in the air we breathe. It makes up four-fifths of the air.

## noble gas, see inert gas

## northern lights, see aurora

## nova

A 'new' star that suddenly appears in the heavens. It is not really new, but is a very faint one that has suddenly become very much brighter.

## nuclear energy

Energy which is given out when atoms split apart (fission) or combine together (fusion). We can harness it in nuclear reactors.

## nuclear reactor

A kind of furnace that uses splitting atoms as fuel. In a reactor atoms of uranium are made to split at a steady rate. The heat produced is removed by a gas or liquid (coolant) and made to turn water into steam. The steam is then used to turn steam turbines. In a nuclear power station the turbines generate electricity.

## nucleus

The solid part at the centre of an atom, around which the electrons circle. It is made up of two kinds of tiny particles—protons and neutrons—bound tightly together.

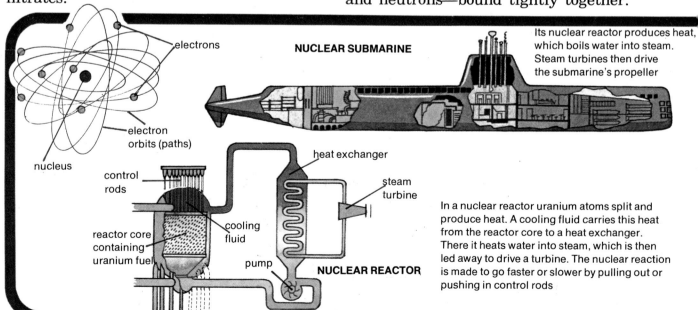

electrons

nucleus

electron orbits (paths)

NUCLEAR SUBMARINE

Its nuclear reactor produces heat, which boils water into steam. Steam turbines then drive the submarine's propeller

control rods

reactor core containing uranium fuel

cooling fluid

pump

heat exchanger

steam turbine

NUCLEAR REACTOR

In a nuclear reactor uranium atoms split and produce heat. A cooling fluid carries this heat from the reactor core to a heat exchanger. There it heats water into steam, which is then led away to drive a turbine. The nuclear reaction is made to go faster or slower by pulling out or pushing in control rods

# Oo

**obsidian,** see **lava**

**oil,** see **petroleum**

## orbit
The path travelled in space when one body circles another. Satellites travel in orbits around the Earth. The Earth and its fellow planets travel in orbits around the Sun.

## ore
A mineral from which a metal can be readily extracted. Bauxite is the ore of aluminium. Haematite is one of several ores of iron.

## organic
Coming from living things. Animal and vegetable matter is organic. It is made up of many different kinds of substances containing carbon. Organic chemistry is the study of carbon compounds.

Every living thing is made up of hundreds of different organic compounds

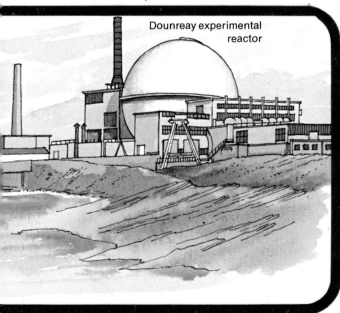

Dounreay experimental reactor

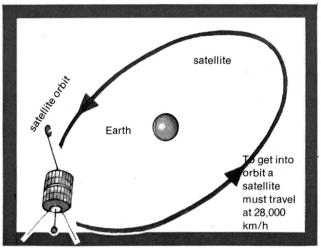

## orrery
A device for showing the movements of the heavenly bodies.

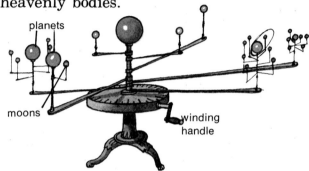

planets
moons
winding handle

## osmium
A metal that is the heaviest of all chemical elements. It is twice as heavy as lead and $22\frac{1}{2}$ times as heavy as water.

## oxidation
What happens when oxygen combines with another element. Burning and rusting are both forms of oxidation. Other elements, including chlorine, have a similar action to oxygen. We also call this oxidation.

## oxygen
The most important of all gases, for it is the one we must breathe to live. It makes up about a fifth of the air. Animals breathe air into their lungs. The oxygen in the air dissolves in the blood in the lung tissue, and the blood carries the oxygen to every cell in the body. Without a constant supply of oxygen the cells would quickly die. Substances combine with oxygen when they burn.

## ozone
A form of oxygen which has three instead of two atoms in its molecules.

41

# Pp

## particle accelerator

A machine used to accelerate atomic particles to very high speeds. The speedy particles are then used to bombard and split atoms. The machine is also called an atom smasher. One kind of accelerator, the cyclotron, accelerates particles in a circle. Another, the linear accelerator, accelerates them in a straight line. The most powerful accelerators use more power than a small town.

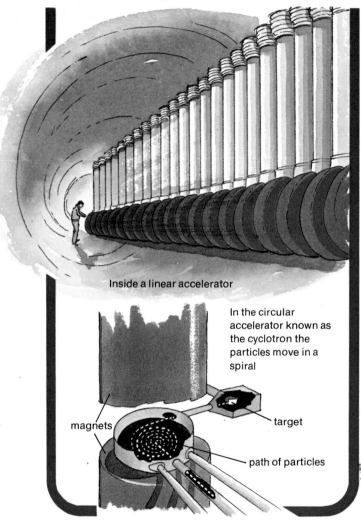

Inside a linear accelerator

In the circular accelerator known as the cyclotron the particles move in a spiral

magnets

target

path of particles

## payload

The object that a space rocket carries into orbit.

## peat

Partly decayed vegetable matter, which is an early stage in the formation of coal. When dried, it can be used as fuel.

## pendulum

A device that swings back and forth at a constant rate. The simplest one is a weight tied to the end of a piece of string. The time it takes a pendulum to swing back and forth depends only on its length. Most clocks once used to be regulated by a pendulum.

This kind of wall clock is often called a grandmother clock. It is much smaller than the grandfather, or long-case clock. Many grandfather clocks have a 'seconds' pendulum 99cm long. It is so called because it makes one swing in exactly one second

## penicillin

The first antibiotic, discovered by Alexander Fleming in 1928.

## periscope

An instrument with which you can look over high walls and round corners. It contains two mirrors which bend the path of light. Submarines use a periscope to see above the surface, while remaining submerged.

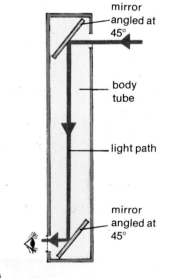

mirror angled at 45°

body tube

light path

mirror angled at 45°

submarine periscope

## persistence of vision

The property our eyes have of holding an image of what they see for a fraction of a second. It makes possible motion pictures, or 'movies'. At the cinema a series of still pictures are shown in rapid succession. Because of the persistence of vision, we see the separate pictures as a moving image.

## petrified forest
The remains, in stone, of an ancient forest. The wood of the trees has literally turned to stone, or petrified.

rocker gear (rocks back and forth to open and close the valves)

cylinder head (holds the valve gear)

valves (open to let fuel in and burnt gases out)

sparking plugs (produce the spark to explode the fuel)

pistons (move up and down in the cylinders)

fan (draws in air)

cylinder block (main part of the engine, containing the cylinders)

camshaft (operates the valves)

flywheel (keeps engine running smoothly)

crankshaft (changes the up and down movements of the pistons into a turning motion)

oil (to lubricate the moving parts)

sump (holds oil)

## petrol engine
The ordinary kind of car engine, which burns petrol as fuel. In the engine the petrol is mixed with air and exploded by a spark. The hot gases formed push pistons down the cylinders, which causes the crankshaft to turn. Movement of the shaft is then carried through gears to the driving wheels. In each cylinder the piston goes through a repeated cycle of four strokes (movements) to produce power. The strokes are as follows:

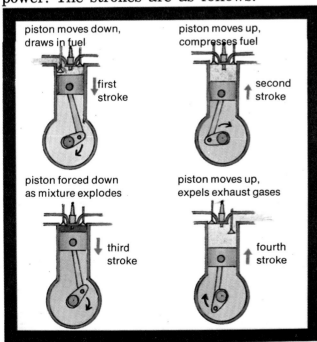

piston moves down, draws in fuel — first stroke

piston moves up, compresses fuel — second stroke

piston forced down as mixture explodes — third stroke

piston moves up, expels exhaust gases — fourth stroke

## petroleum
Oil which is found trapped in the rocks. From it we can extract petrol, kerosene, engine oils and greases, together with many kinds of useful chemicals. Petroleum is a mixture of hydrocarbons. They are separated into useful products by refining.

offshore oil rig

## phases of the Moon

The changes in shape of the Moon which we see from the Earth. The Moon does not change in shape of course. What does change is the amount of its surface lit by the Sun.

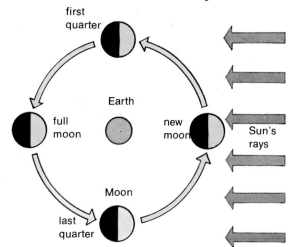

## photography

'Writing with light'. Taking pictures on a film with a camera. The first photograph was taken on a pewter plate covered with bitumen in about 1826. Modern photographs are taken on a clear plastic strip, coated with silver salts.

## photosynthesis

The chemical process by which green plants make food. They take in carbon dioxide from the air and water from the ground and use the energy in sunlight to change the carbon dioxide and water into sugar.

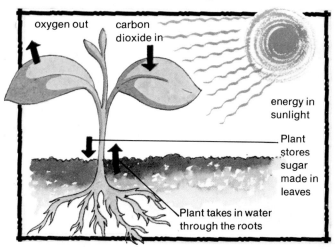

## physics

The study of the properties of matter and energy. Physicists study heat, light, sound, electricity and magnetism. They also study forces and the way they affect objects.

## planet

A heavenly body that circles around the Sun. The Earth is a planet. There are eight other planets. Going out from the Sun, they are Mercury, Venus, (Earth), Mars, Jupiter, Saturn, Uranus, Neptune and Pluto. Jupiter, Saturn, Uranus and Neptune are made up mainly of gas. The other planets are rocky, like the Earth.

## plastics

Substances with long molecules which can be easily shaped by heat. Most of them are made from chemicals obtained from petroleum. Among the commonest plastics are polythene, PVC (polyvinylchloride), nylon and polystyrene. Note that many of these names begin with 'poly'. 'Poly' means 'many', and the long molecules of these plastics are made up of many smaller molecules joined together. There are many ways of making plastic goods. Many are made by injecting or blowing molten plastic into moulds. Plastic fibres are now widely used to make clothing fabrics.

## platinum

A rare white metal more precious than gold. It is used in making jewellery for it is hard and keeps its shine. It is used in industry as a catalyst, for example, in refining petroleum.

## Pluto

The most distant of the planets, which lies about 6,000 million kilometres away. It is a tiny ice-covered lump of rock, maybe even smaller than the planet Mercury. It was not discovered until 1930.

## plutonium

A radioactive and very poisonous metal. It does not occur naturally on Earth. It has been made by scientists in the laboratory by bombarding the metal uranium with atomic particles.

## pole star, Polaris

The star which is located almost directly above the Earth's North Pole. Because of this, its position in the night sky scarcely changes at all. All the other stars wheel overhead because the Earth is spinning.

## pollution

Poisoning of the air, water and land. Dangerous fumes from car engines and chimneys help pollute the air. Chemical wastes and oil pollute the rivers and seas. Other pollution may be caused by spraying crops with insecticides and weed-killers.

## power

Rate of working. It often used to be expressed in horsepower—the rate at which a horse could work. Inventor James Watt devised this term, and the unit of electrical power—the watt—is now named after him.

## pressure

The force acting over a unit area—say, 1 square centimetre—of something. The pressure of the air on the surface of the Earth is about 1 kilogram per square centimetre. The total force acting on a surface equals the pressure times the area of the surface.

## prism, see spectrum

Stars arc around Polaris in a long-exposure photograph

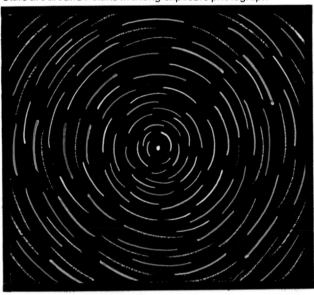

cellulose acetate handles

fibreglass case

PVC disc

polystyrene beaker

soft polythene 'squeeze' bottle

polythene bag

WASH

synthetic rubber boots

Polaroid lenses

Orlon sweater

Nylon coat

Crimplene trousers

PVC guttering

non-stick coating

Bakelite handle

PVC hose

polythene toys

hard polythene bowl

## probe

A spacecraft that ventures into deep space to explore the Moon (lunar probe) and the planets (planetary probe). Probes carry many kinds of measuring instruments and often cameras to take close-up pictures. They may be powered by solar or nuclear batteries.

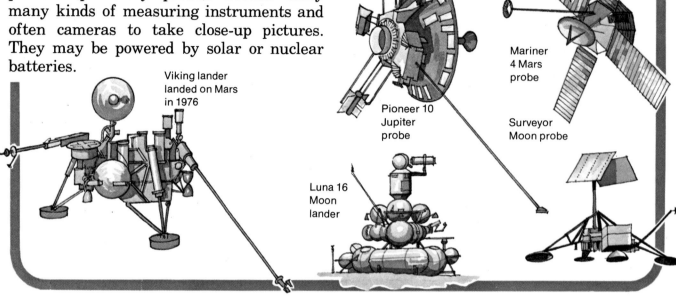

Viking lander landed on Mars in 1976

Pioneer 10 Jupiter probe

Mariner 4 Mars probe

solar cells

Surveyor Moon probe

Luna 16 Moon lander

### propellant, see rocket

### protein

One of our main food substances, which goes to build up our body tissues. Important sources of protein are lean meat, fish, milk, cheese and eggs.

### proton

One of the two main particles found within the nucleus of all atoms. It has a positive electric charge.

### Proxima Centauri

The star closest to the Earth. It is a very faint red star in the constellation of Centaurus. It lies a little over $4\frac{1}{4}$ light-years away.

### pulley

A simple machine consisting of a wheel and a rope which enables us to lift heavy loads more easily. A block-and-tackle is made up of several pulleys linked together.

### pulsar

A tiny but very heavy star which spins rapidly and gives out its energy in rapid and very powerful pulses (bursts).

### pump

A mechanical device for moving a liquid or a gas through a pipe. We use a bicycle pump to pump air into the tyres. We use a lift pump to pump water from a well. Car engines have what is known as a gear pump to pump oil to the moving parts.

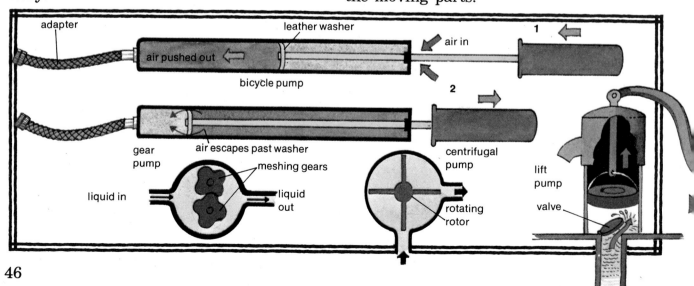

adapter

leather washer

air in

1

air pushed out

bicycle pump

2

gear pump

air escapes past washer

centrifugal pump

lift pump

liquid in

meshing gears

liquid out

rotating rotor

valve

# Qq

## quartz

A common mineral, found in many different forms. Its chemical name is silica, or silicon dioxide. Ordinary sand is made up of tiny grains of quartz. Some quartz crystals are valued as gemstones, including amethyst, cairngorm and rose quartz.

## quasar

A mysterious heavenly body which gives out strong radio waves. Quasars appear to be hundreds of times smaller than galaxies but give out the light of hundreds of galaxies. They also appear to be a very long way away.

## quicksilver, see mercury

# Rr

## radar

Using radio waves to find the position of objects. Pulses (bursts) of short radio waves (microwaves) are sent out and are reflected by objects in their path. From the returned 'echoes' the range and direction of the object can be found. 'Radar' is short for 'radio detection and ranging'.

## radiation

The way in which things give off energy. The Sun, for example, gives off energy as light and heat, which are both forms of radiation. Uranium gives off radiation from its atoms —atomic radiation. Atomic radiation is very penetrating and can kill living things.

## radio

Certain waves—radio waves—can be made to 'carry' sound signals. These radio carrier waves can then be transmitted. A radio receiver picks up these waves with its aerial. Its electrical circuits then sort out, or detect the sound signals and change them back into sound.

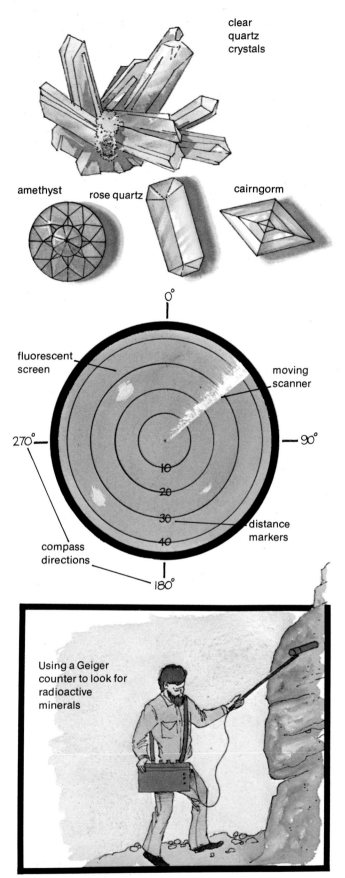

clear quartz crystals

amethyst    rose quartz    cairngorm

fluorescent screen
moving scanner
compass directions
distance markers

Using a Geiger counter to look for radioactive minerals

## radioactivity

The atoms of some chemical elements constantly break down and give out radiation. This behaviour is called radioactivity.

47

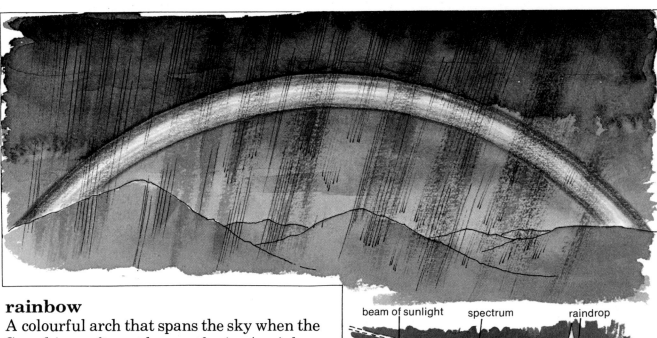

## rainbow

A colourful arch that spans the sky when the Sun shines after a shower of rain. A rainbow appears when the Sun is shining behind you, and it is raining in front of you. The raindrops act like tiny prisms and split up sunlight into a spectrum.

## reaction

This has two main meanings. (1) In chemistry a reaction is what takes place when chemicals combine together. (2) In physics, reaction is a force. Whenever one force is acting, another equal force (reaction) is acting against it in the opposite direction.

When you go to step out of a boat...

...reaction makes the boat go backwards as you go forwards

**reactor,** see **nuclear reactor**

## red giant

A huge reddish star very much bigger than the Sun. The biggest stars are called super-giants. One day, thousands of millions of years hence, the Sun will become a red giant.

beam of sunlight    spectrum    raindrop

## refining

Purifying something. Metals are refined after they have been extracted from their ores. This takes place in furnaces. Petroleum is refined after it is mined. A refinery separates the oil into its different parts.

petroleum refinery

## reflection

What happens when light, sound or other waves bounce back from a surface. Sound reflections are called echoes.

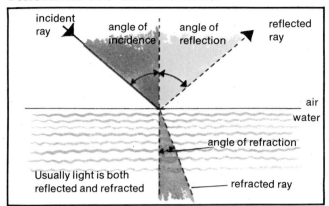

## refraction

The bending of light when it passes from one substance into another—for example, from air into glass or water.

## refrigerator

A device that keeps food cold. It works by changing a liquid into a vapour. Cooling occurs whenever this happens.

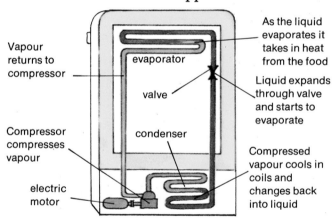

Vapour returns to compressor

evaporator

valve

condenser

Compressor compresses vapour

electric motor

As the liquid evaporates it takes in heat from the food

Liquid expands through valve and starts to evaporate

Compressed vapour cools in coils and changes back into liquid

## relativity

A complicated theory that explains how energy, matter, space, time and motion are related. It was suggested by Albert Einstein.

## rocket

A powerful motor that works by jet propulsion. A rocket burns its fuel inside a chamber to produce hot gases. These shoot backwards out of a nozzle and propel the rocket forwards by reaction. A rocket differs from a jet engine because it carries its own oxygen supply. Both the fuel and the oxygen supplies are called propellants. The most powerful rockets use liquid propellants.

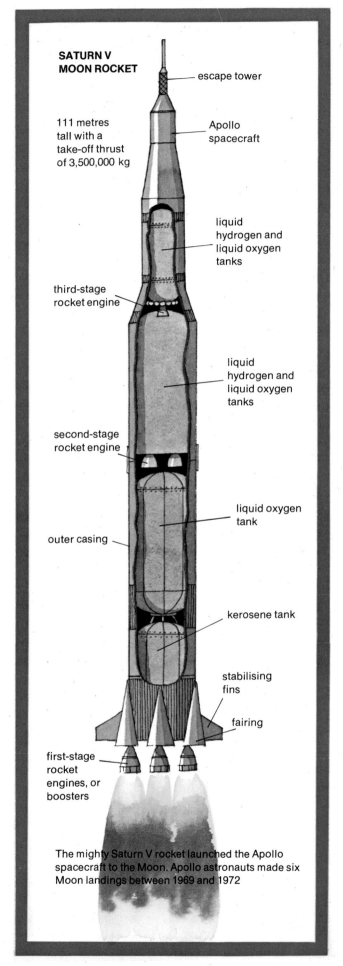

SATURN V MOON ROCKET

escape tower

Apollo spacecraft

111 metres tall with a take-off thrust of 3,500,000 kg

liquid hydrogen and liquid oxygen tanks

third-stage rocket engine

liquid hydrogen and liquid oxygen tanks

second-stage rocket engine

liquid oxygen tank

outer casing

kerosene tank

stabilising fins

fairing

first-stage rocket engines, or boosters

The mighty Saturn V rocket launched the Apollo spacecraft to the Moon. Apollo astronauts made six Moon landings between 1969 and 1972

weathered granite

limestone outcrop

slate quarry

## rocks

Three kinds of rock make up the Earth's crust—igneous, sedimentary and metamorphic. *Igneous rocks* (basalt, granite) were formed when molten rock cooled on or near the surface. *Sedimentary rocks* (chalk, limestone) were formed from layers of broken-down rocks. *Metamorphic rocks* (slate, marble) were formed when molten rock changed existing rock.

## rust

A brownish-orange substance that forms on iron and steel left out in the rain. It is iron oxide.

# Ss

## saccharin

A chemical made from oil or coal which is 500 times sweeter than sugar.

## salt

A common mineral, found in large quantities in the sea. Its chemical name is sodium chloride. It is one of a class of chemicals called salts. In general salts are formed when an acid combines with an alkali: acid+alkali=salt+water.

## sand

Finely ground rock. It is created at the seaside, for example, by the action of the waves. The most common mineral in sand is quartz.

## satellite

A tiny body, which circles around a planet; a moon. Around the Earth there are now many man-made moons, or artificial satellites.

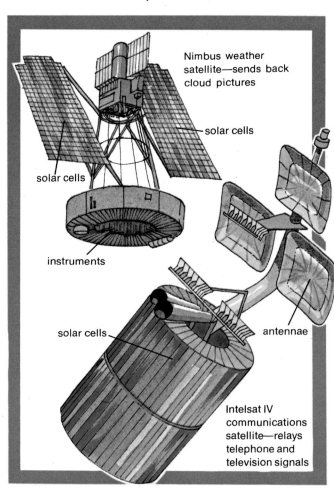

Nimbus weather satellite—sends back cloud pictures

solar cells

solar cells

instruments

solar cells

antennae

Intelsat IV communications satellite—relays telephone and television signals

## Saturn

The second largest planet in the solar system, famous for its beautiful rings. About 120,000 km in diameter, it is mainly gaseous, like Jupiter. It has at least 14 moons circling around it.

## science

The word simply means 'knowing' or 'knowledge', and scientists search for knowledge of the world about them. There are many branches of science. This book is concerned with the *physical sciences*—chemistry, physics, astronomy and geology. They investigate the nature of the universe, from tiny atoms to vast galaxies. The other main branches of science are the *biological sciences* botany and zoology; and the *social sciences,* which include such things as anthropology (the study of different peoples) and economics.

## seasons

The regular changes in climate that occur during the year. The changes come about because the Earth's axis is tilted in space. Places on Earth are hottest when they are tilted most towards the Sun (in summer). They are coldest when they are tilted most away from the Sun (in winter).

## sedimentary rock, see rocks

## seismology

The study of earthquakes. Seismologists record the pressure waves (seismic waves) set up in the ground by earthquakes with a seismograph.

## semiconductor

A material like silicon that conducts (passes on) electricity only very slightly; used in modern electronic devices, often in the form of tiny, wafer-thin 'chips'.

## shooting star, see meteor

## silica

The commonest substance in the Earth's crust, chemically known as silicon dioxide. Quartz is the best-known form of silica.

the ringed planet Saturn

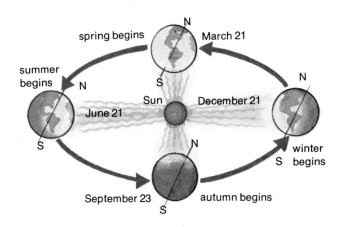

The diagram shows four points in the path of the Earth around the Sun each year. The northern hemisphere is tilted most towards the Sun on about 21 June and enjoys summer; and is tilted most away on about 21 December and suffers winter

## silver

A white precious metal found native (in metal form) in the Earth's crust. It can be shaped very easily and made into beautiful objects. Silver was probably discovered by prehistoric man after gold and copper.

## siphon

A tube that carries liquid from a higher to a lower level. Siphon action is used, for example, in the flush toilet (water closet). It works because of air pressure.

## Sirius
The brightest star in the sky, in the constellation Canis Major, the Great Dog.

## smelting
Heating an ore in a furnace to extract the metal it contains.

## snow
Tiny feathery masses of ice crystals that fall from the clouds when the air is cold.

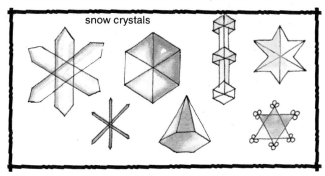
snow crystals

## soap
A cleansing substance made by boiling fat with an alkali, usually caustic soda.

## soda
The name given to some common chemicals containing sodium. Washing soda is sodium carbonate. Baking soda is sodium bicarbonate. Caustic soda is sodium hydroxide.

## solar
Of the Sun; from the Latin word *sol,* meaning 'Sun'.

## solar cell
A device that changes sunlight into electricity. Spacecraft are powered by panels containing solar cells.

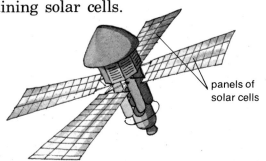
panels of solar cells

## solar system
The family of bodies that circles around the Sun. Its most important members are the nine planets, including the Earth, and their moons. It also includes the wide 'belt' of asteroids, together with the comets and the rocky lumps we see as meteors. The picture shows the orbits of the planets in their relative positions. But neither the orbits nor the planets are drawn to scale.

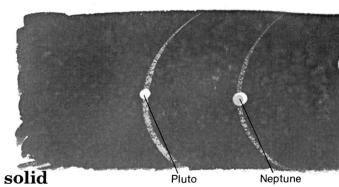
Pluto    Neptune

## solid
One of the three main states of matter. Solids have a definite shape and size.

## solution
What results when you dissolve a substance in a liquid. The substance being dissolved is called the *solute.* The dissolving liquid is called the *solvent.*

## sonar
Detecting objects by means of sound waves. Bats use sonar to detect obstacles in their path. They emit high-pitched squeaks and listen for the echoes.

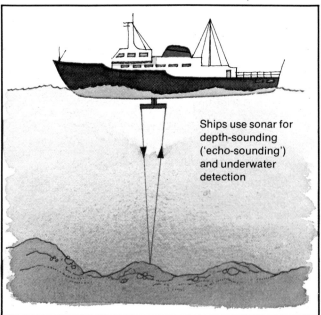
Ships use sonar for depth-sounding ('echo-sounding') and underwater detection

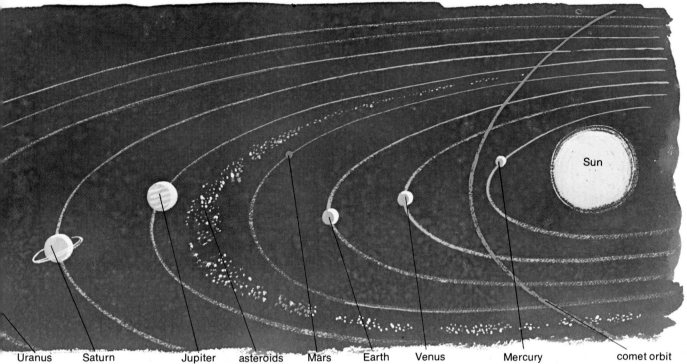

Uranus    Saturn          Jupiter    asteroids    Mars    Earth    Venus         Mercury              comet orbit

## sound

Vibrations in the air which we hear as sound when they strike our ears. The vibrations are passed on by the air molecules moving back and forth. Sound waves travel at about 1,200 km per hour.

## Soyuz

The Russian spacecraft used to ferry cosmonauts to and from orbit.

## space

The emptiness that exists between the planets and the stars. It is an almost perfect vacuum.

## space shuttle

A craft that can make many journeys to and from space. It takes off like a rocket but lands like a plane. The Russians call their shuttle Kosmolyot.

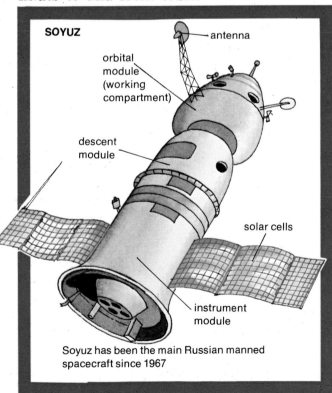

**SOYUZ**

antenna

orbital module (working compartment)

descent module

solar cells

instrument module

Soyuz has been the main Russian manned spacecraft since 1967

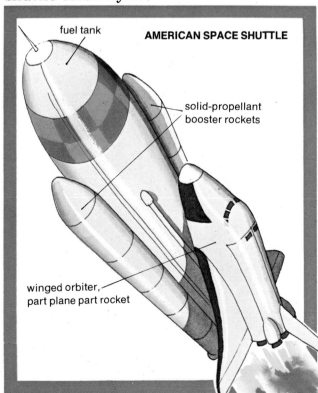

fuel tank        **AMERICAN SPACE SHUTTLE**

solid-propellant booster rockets

winged orbiter, part plane part rocket

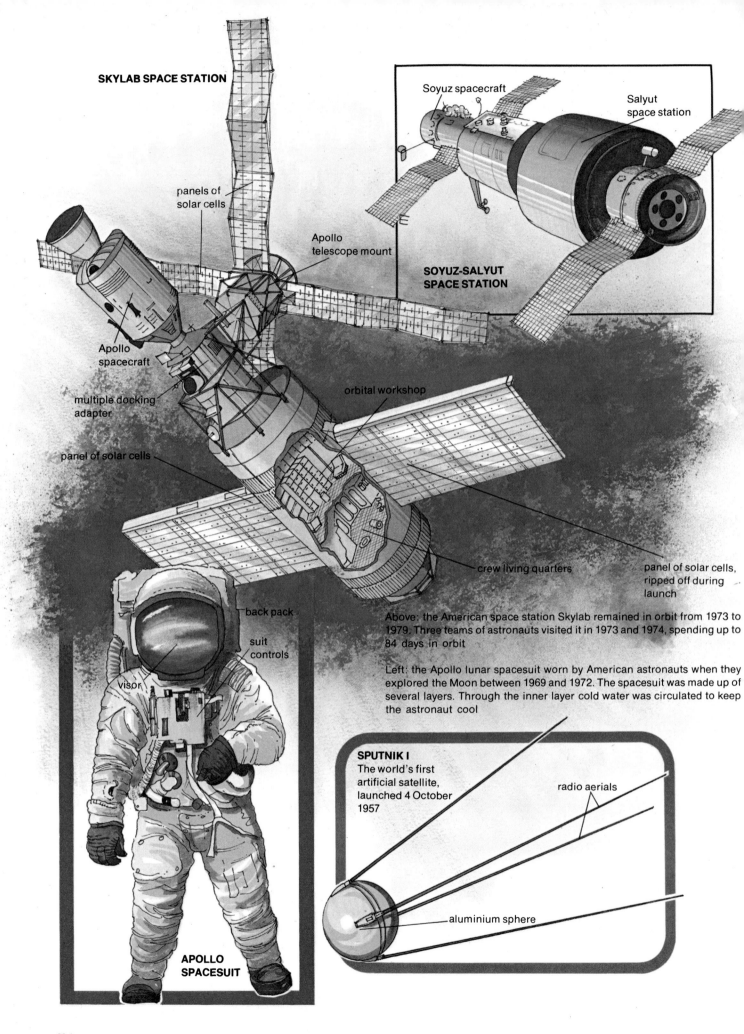

**SKYLAB SPACE STATION**

panels of solar cells

Apollo telescope mount

Apollo spacecraft

multiple docking adapter

panel of solar cells

orbital workshop

crew living quarters

panel of solar cells, ripped off during launch

Soyuz spacecraft

Salyut space station

**SOYUZ-SALYUT SPACE STATION**

Above: the American space station Skylab remained in orbit from 1973 to 1979. Three teams of astronauts visited it in 1973 and 1974, spending up to 84 days in orbit

Left: the Apollo lunar spacesuit worn by American astronauts when they explored the Moon between 1969 and 1972. The spacesuit was made up of several layers. Through the inner layer cold water was circulated to keep the astronaut cool

back pack

suit controls

visor

**APOLLO SPACESUIT**

**SPUTNIK I**
The world's first artificial satellite, launched 4 October 1957

radio aerials

aluminium sphere

## space station
A large structure built in orbit, in which astronauts can live for months at a time.

## spacesuit
A suit astronauts wear when they leave their spacecraft and go into space. It gives them oxygen to breathe, keeps them cool and protects them from particles and radiation.

## spectrum
The band of colour obtained when white light is split up by a prism. Raindrops act in a similar way to produce a rainbow.

## sputnik
The Russian term for a space satellite.

## stalactites and stalagmites
Formations that occur in limestone caves. Stalactites are columns hanging from the roof. Stalagmites rise from the floor. They grow as dripping water deposits the lime it contains. (See the picture on the right.)

## star
A huge ball of hot, glowing gas, which shines in space. Our Sun is a star. The other stars lie millions upon millions of kilometres away in space—so far that their light takes years to reach us. Even in the largest telescopes they appear only as tiny points of light.

## states of matter
Everything on Earth exists either as a gas, a liquid or a solid. These are the three main states of matter. Scientists now recognize a fourth state, called plasma. This exists in the searing-hot interior of stars, where atoms are stripped of their electrons.

## static electricity
A kind of electricity which exists around an object with an electric charge. A comb can be given static electricity simply by combing the hair.

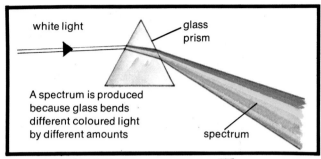

white light

glass prism

A spectrum is produced because glass bends different coloured light by different amounts

spectrum

## steam
Water in the form of a gas. Water changes into steam when it boils. Steam engines use the force of expanding steam to produce power. Steam we can see contains minute droplets of water.

## steel
An alloy of iron, containing traces of carbon and other metals. It is made by refining impure iron in a furnace.

## stellar
Of the stars; from the Latin *stella,* 'a star'.

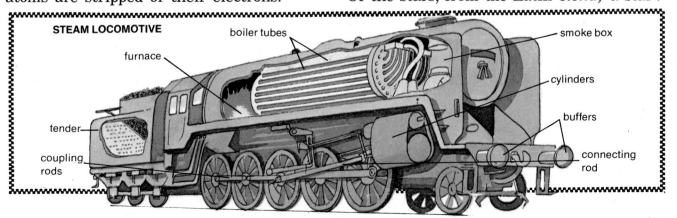

STEAM LOCOMOTIVE

boiler tubes

smoke box

furnace

cylinders

tender

buffers

coupling rods

connecting rod

## step rocket

A space rocket consisting of several rockets joined together, one on top of the other.

## streamlining

Shaping an object so that it slips easily through the air or through the water.

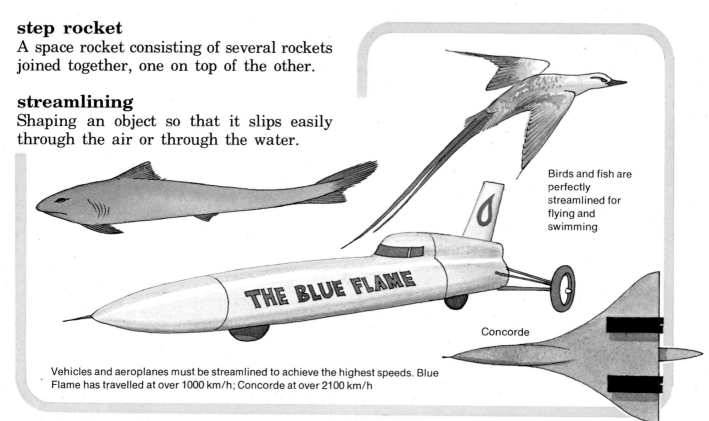

Birds and fish are perfectly streamlined for flying and swimming

Concorde

Vehicles and aeroplanes must be streamlined to achieve the highest speeds. Blue Flame has travelled at over 1000 km/h; Concorde at over 2100 km/h

## sulphuric acid

A very strong acid which is perhaps the most important chemical in industry. It is used in thousands of chemical processes. It forms salts called sulphates.

## Sun

Our star, which lies about 150 million kilometres away in space. It is the centre of the solar system, around which the Earth and the other planets circle. It measures about 140,000 km across.

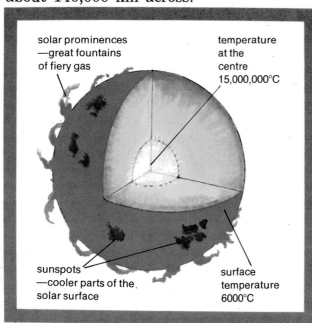

solar prominences —great fountains of fiery gas

temperature at the centre 15,000,000°C

sunspots —cooler parts of the solar surface

surface temperature 6000°C

## superconductor

A metal with no resistance to electricity. A few rare metals become superconductors at very low temperatures (about −270°C).

## supernova

A star that suddenly gets many times brighter and blows itself apart.

## supersonic

Faster than the speed of sound (about 1,200 km per hour). Aircraft speeds are expressed in Mach numbers; Mach 1 is the speed of sound; Mach 2 is twice the speed of sound.

## surface tension

A force at the surface of a liquid, which gives it a kind of 'skin'.

needles floating on the surface 'skin' of water

## synthetic

Not natural. Made from chemicals produced in factories. As in synthetic fibres.

# Tt

## telephone

A means of sending voice messages through wires over long distances. The sound of the voice is changed into electrical signals in the mouthpiece, or microphone. The signals travel through the telephone wires to the receiver's earpiece, which is a miniature loudspeaker. There they are changed back into sounds.

In the earpiece of the person you are talking to the electrical signals go to an electromagnet which vibrates a diaphragm to make sounds

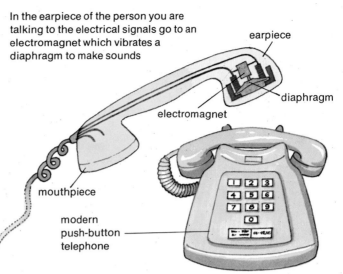

earpiece
diaphragm
electromagnet
mouthpiece
modern push-button telephone

When you speak into the mouthpiece, the diaphragm vibrates and sets up electrical signals in the wires

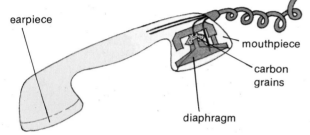

earpiece
mouthpiece
carbon grains
diaphragm

## telescope

The instrument astronomers use to look at the heavenly bodies. It makes things look bigger or brighter. Some telescopes (refractors) have lenses; others (reflectors) have mirrors to gather and focus the light.

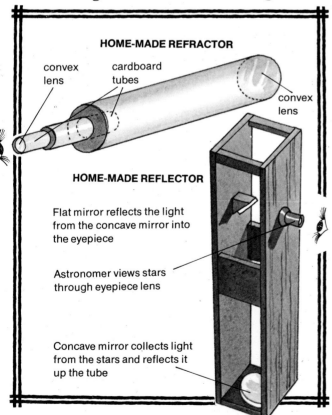

**HOME-MADE REFRACTOR**

convex lens
cardboard tubes
convex lens

**HOME-MADE REFLECTOR**

Flat mirror reflects the light from the concave mirror into the eyepiece

Astronomer views stars through eyepiece lens

Concave mirror collects light from the stars and reflects it up the tube

## television, see cathode-ray tube

## temperature

The 'hotness' of something, measured by a thermometer. It is measured in degrees on a scale called the Celsius, or centigrade scale. On this scale water freezes at 0° and boils at 100°. Temperature used to be measured on the Fahrenheit (F) scale—on that scale water freezes at 32° and boils at 212°. The temperature of a healthy human body is around 37.0°C.

temperature scales
alcohol
thermometer bulb

## terrestrial

Of the Earth; from the Latin word for Earth, *Terra*.

## thermometer

An instrument that measures temperature. The ordinary home thermometer contains a column of liquid which gets longer or shorter as the temperature goes up and down. The liquid is usually coloured alcohol or mercury.

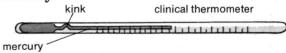

kink
clinical thermometer
mercury

## thermostat

A switch that turns on and off as necessary to keep the temperature of something constant.

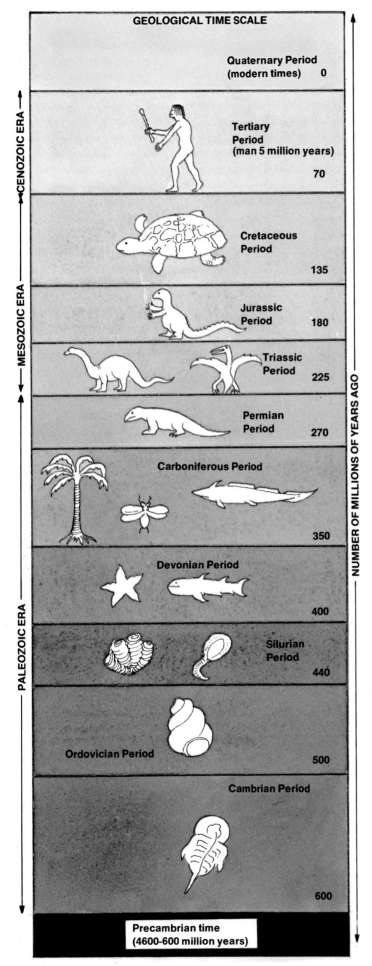

### GEOLOGICAL TIME SCALE

CENOZOIC ERA

Quaternary Period
(modern times)    0

Tertiary
Period
(man 5 million years)

70

Cretaceous
Period

135

Jurassic
Period    180

Triassic
Period
225

MESOZOIC ERA

Permian
Period

270

Carboniferous Period

350

PALEOZOIC ERA

Devonian Period

400

Silurian
Period

440

Ordovician Period

500

Cambrian Period

600

NUMBER OF MILLIONS OF YEARS AGO

Precambrian time
(4600-600 million years)

## thunder
The noise that accompanies a lightning flash. The flash heats the air, which suddenly expands and makes a noise like an explosion.

## tidal wave
A huge wave triggered off by an earthquake under the sea. It is properly called a tsunami, and is nothing to do with the tides.

## tide
The regular rise and fall of the sea, which occurs about every 12 hours. Tides are caused mainly by the Moon, which tends to pull the oceans towards it by its gravity.

## time
We usually measure time from the motion of the Earth in space. Our day is the time it takes the Earth to spin once on its axis. Our year is the time it takes the Earth to make one journey around the Sun. One year $= 365\frac{1}{4}$ days. On this scale, the Earth is about 4,600 million years old. Little is known about the first 4,000 million years of the Earth's history. But we know something about the past 600 million years from the fossils found in the rocks formed during this time. These fossils help us build up a geological time scale (left), split into eras and periods.

## tornado
A powerful wind-storm in which the wind spirals round and round at fantastic speeds. It devastates everything in its path.

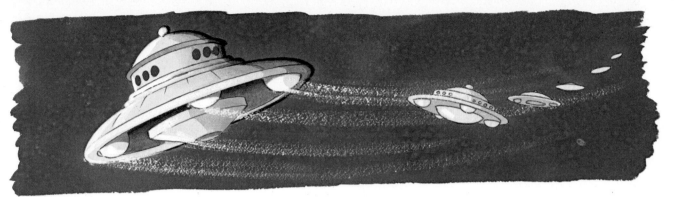

## transformer

An electrical device which increases or decreases electrical voltage. It consists of two coils of wire wound around an iron core.

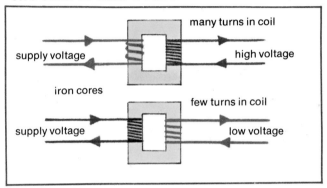

many turns in coil

supply voltage

high voltage

iron cores

few turns in coil

supply voltage

low voltage

## transistor

A tiny crystal chip which can change and amplify (strengthen) electric current passing through it. It is used in all kinds of modern electronic devices, such as pocket radios.

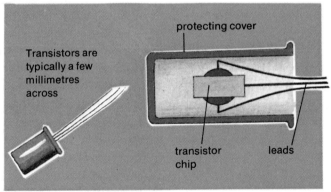

Transistors are typically a few millimetres across

protecting cover

transistor chip

leads

## transmutation

Changing one chemical element into another. This can be done by bombarding the element with atomic particles.

## tsunami, see tidal wave

## tungsten

A hard metal which has the highest melting point of all the chemical elements, 3,410°C. The filament wire in light bulbs is made of tungsten.

'flying saucer' UFO

# Uu

## UFO

Short for Unidentified Flying Object. Some people believe that UFOs come from another world, but there is no evidence of this.

## ultrasonics

The study of sound waves so high pitched that the human ear cannot hear them. Bats emit ultrasonic waves to help them navigate.

## ultraviolet rays

Invisible radiation that comes from the Sun. It is these rays that tan our bodies in summer.

## universe

Space and all there is in it—stars, planets, moons and so on. The universe is believed to be about 15,000 million years old.

## uranium

A rare radioactive metal used as 'fuel' in nuclear reactors. It is unusual among the elements because its atoms can be made to split (fission) quite easily.

## Uranus

A distant planet made up mainly of gas. It is about 50,000 km in diameter, and has a faint ring system around it, like Saturn. Uranus was discovered in 1781 by William Herschel.

# VWXYZ

## vacuum

A space from which the air has been removed. A near perfect vacuum exists in space, between the planets and the stars.

## vacuum flask

Also called Thermos and Dewar flask. It is a glass vessel made with double walls, which have a vacuum between them. It can keep hot liquids hot and cold liquids cold.

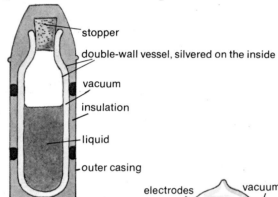

- stopper
- double-wall vessel, silvered on the inside
- vacuum
- insulation
- liquid
- outer casing

## valve

Also called vacuum tube. A device used in electronics to amplify (strengthen) and control electric current; now often replaced by a transistor.

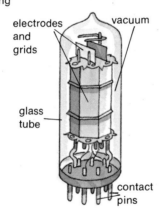

electrodes and grids

vacuum

glass tube

contact pins

## vapour

What liquids turn into when they are heated; a gas.

## Venus

The planet closest to Earth and Earth's near twin in size. Its diameter is about 12,140 km. It is permanently covered by cloud.

## volcano

An opening in the Earth's crust through which molten rock escapes as lava, in one of nature's great firework displays.

## water

Our most precious liquid, without which life would be impossible. It is a compound of hydrogen and oxygen which we write as $H_2O$. This means that every molecule of water contains two hydrogen atoms and one oxygen atom.

Water evaporates from the oceans

Water vapour condenses to form a cloud of water droplets

Water evaporates from the land

Cross-section of a volcano, showing the molten rock forcing its way through the rock layers

## water cycle

The regular exchange of water between the ground (evaporation) and the atmosphere (rainfall). About 500 million million tonnes of water pass between the two every year. See diagram below.

## weight

Heaviness; a measure of the pull on an object due to gravity. It is different from mass. An object always has mass, but it only has weight when gravity acts on it.

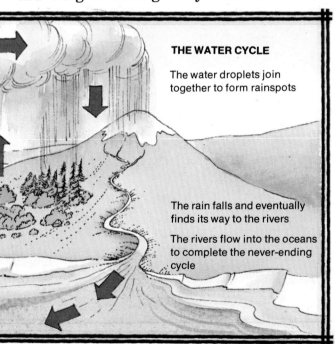

**THE WATER CYCLE**

The water droplets join together to form rainspots

The rain falls and eventually finds its way to the rivers

The rivers flow into the oceans to complete the never-ending cycle

## weightlessness

A state which astronauts experience in a spacecraft in orbit. They have no weight because there is no gravity in orbit.

## white dwarf

A star near the end of its life. It is small and very dense—a teaspoonful of its matter would weigh many tonnes.

## X-rays

Very penetrating radiation, which can pass easily through flesh but not bones. Body photographs taken with X-rays show the bone structure.

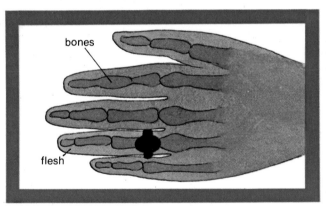

bones

flesh

## year

The time it takes the Earth to circle the Sun—$365\frac{1}{4}$ days. The odd $\frac{1}{4}$ day makes it necessary to add an extra day to one calendar year (leap year) in four.

## zodiac

The constellations the Sun and the planets appear to pass through during the year.

## zoology

The study of animals; one of the two main branches of biology.